The Old Testament Made Simple

An Overview
With Discussion Questions

Part 1 – Genesis through 2 Samuel 13

by Don Davidson, B.A., J.D.

CFT Publishing

Bedford, Texas

Published by CFT Publishing
Bedford, Texas
ISBN 978-0-9992335-4-2

Other books by Don Davidson:

Beyond Blind Faith: Reasons For the Hope We Have (1 Peter 3:15), available on Amazon.com.

Beyond Shallow Faith: Cultivating Christian Maturity (Ephesians 4:13-15), available on Amazon.com.

For more information on these books and other writings by Don, including his blog and some free downloadable stories, visit *dondavidson.net*.

You can contact Don via email at *donatty@flash.net*.

TABLE OF CONTENTS

Table of Contents

Table of Contents

Table of Contents

Table of Contents

Preface

After I became a Christian at age twenty, I tried to read the Old Testament and found large portions of it to be almost incomprehensible. Yahweh—also translated as "Jehovah"—seemed much different from the Heavenly Father Jesus talked about. Indeed, Yahweh seems so different that some early Christians insisted he could not possibly be the same God that we see in the New Testament. Some Christians today seem to feel the same way, as do many non-Christians.

Yet with time and education from some older and wiser Christians—none more influential than the late Dr. Gene Scott—I came to understand and appreciate the lessons Yahweh was trying to teach his people. (Dr. Eugene Scott was for many years the pastor of Faith Center in Glendale, California. That is where I began listening to his teaching.) He is the same Heavenly Father that Jesus talked about, but in the Old Testament Yahweh was dealing with people who were at a much different level of spiritual maturity than those of Jesus' time. That difference made all the difference.

This book, in combination with Part 2, explores each book of the Protestant Old Testament except Psalms, Proverbs, Ecclesiastes, and Song of Solomon.

Each short chapter provides a synopsis of a significant topic or storyline in the Old Testament, and includes thought-provoking—and discussion-provoking—questions. Most of these questions have no right or wrong answer. Some may be impossible to answer, but are nevertheless worth thinking or talking about.

This book did not require a lot of biblical interpretation, since I am mostly conveying what the Old Testament *says* rather than what it *means*. Nevertheless, some interpretation was necessary—perhaps more than I realize. So I will share my philosophy on interpreting scripture. I primarily rely upon two rules.

I borrowed the first one from the law—the doctrine of *pari materia* (Latin for "on the same subject"). This rule recognizes that lawmakers do not intentionally pass laws that contradict each other, and therefore an interpretation which leads to that result is probably wrong. This doctrine requires courts to interpret laws so that they are consistent with each other whenever possible, so long as they address the same general subject or have the same general purpose.

A similar approach is useful in biblical interpretation. We can be reasonably certain that the Old Testament writers did not intend to contradict themselves or each other. Because I believe that those authors honestly reported what they knew or believed to be true, I make every effort to reconcile scriptures that might appear to be in conflict.

The second rule I follow is that every verse should be interpreted in light of the context in which it appears. What was the author's main point? Who was his audience? In some cases, when and where was the book written? What do the verses preceding and following that verse talk about? We will get much closer to a verse's true meaning if we understand the context in which it appears.

Some of the chapters in this book cover only a chapter—or even less—of the Old Testament, while others are drawn from multiple chapters or multiple Old Testament books. Each chapter of this book lists the Old Testament source(s)—under the chapter title—from which it is derived. When the sources include multiple books of the Old Testament, I have provided abundant footnotes so that those who wish to grade my homework, or simply delve more deeply, can easily do so. I have generally omitted footnotes when the chapter relies on a single Old Testament book, unless I am using a direct quote or providing additional information from outside that source. If you believe the extensive footnotes in some of the chapters interfere with your reading enjoyment, I sincerely apologize. I simply feel that the clarity they often provide is worth the minor inconvenience.

All biblical quotations in this book are from the New American Standard Bible (NASB) translation. *Italics* are in the original, and indicate that the word is implied in—but not literally part of—the original Hebrew. You will also notice that "Lord" almost always appears herein with small capitals—LORD—when it is in a quotation from the Old Testament. This is how the NASB renders it, so I have retained that style in the quotations. Similarly, while modern usage no longer uses capital letters for pronouns that refer to God or Jesus Christ, the NASB does, and I have retained that style in the quotations.

Chapter 1
Adam and Eve
(Genesis 2:7–3:24)

When I was a baby Christian, more than 40 years ago, I read the New Testament straight through and found myself agreeing with virtually everything it said. The New Testament seemed to be all about love and mercy and forgiveness. Who could quarrel with that?

Then I bravely set out to read the Old Testament, and never made it out of the Pentateuch. (The Pentateuch consists of the first five books of the Bible: Genesis, Exodus, Leviticus, Numbers, and Deuteronomy.) I didn't understand a lot of it, and it was frankly torpedoing my faith. So I stopped.

Not until years later did I learn what I believe is one of the keys to understanding the Old Testament—trust. So let's start with the story of Adam and Eve, because that story is all about trust.

Now I don't care whether you believe this story is history, allegory, parable, legend, or fable. The story teaches a very important truth.

God gave Adam and Eve one, and only one, rule: don't eat from the tree of the knowledge of good and evil. And he also explained the consequences of disobedience: "you will surely die."[1]

Then along came the serpent probing for weakness: "Indeed, has God said, 'You shall not eat from any tree of the garden'?"[2]

---

1. Genesis 2:17
2. Genesis 3:1

1

Eve knew that the fruit of only one tree was forbidden, but she misremembered God's one rule, because she said: "God has said, 'You shall not eat from it or touch it, or you will die.' "[3] God said nothing about touching it.

So the serpent sowed the seeds of doubt: "You surely will not die!"[4] At this point I imagine the serpent touching the fruit to prove his point. Then he added temptation to doubt: "You will be like God."[5] And Eve was lost.

Eve trusted the serpent instead of God, and she ate. Then Adam trusted Eve instead of God, and he ate. Thus, Adam and Eve failed their lesson in trust. And they eventually died, just as God said they would. But more importantly, they were separated from his presence in the garden, which was their *spiritual* death.

So began mankind's lessons in trusting God. There would be many more.

Questions to ponder or discuss: What are some of the doubts and temptations we face today? How do we overcome them?

---

3. Genesis 3:2-3

4. Genesis 3:4

5. Genesis 3:5

Chapter 2
The Creation Story
(Genesis 1:1–2:3)

Let me frankly state that I am not a Young Earth believer. I cannot accept the idea that Earth is less than 10,000 years old when scientists estimate it is actually billions of years old.

I know Genesis 1 says that God created the world and everything in it in six days, but what is a "day"? We measure a day by the rising and setting of the Sun, but the Sun and Moon weren't created until the fourth day.

2 Peter 3:8 says, "But do not let this one *fact* escape your notice, beloved, that with the Lord one day is like a thousand years, and a thousand years like one day." (Psalm 90:4 is similar.) Time means nothing to God because he doesn't grow up, grow old, or die. A day or a million years makes little difference to him. Genesis 1 talks about six "days" because that was a concept the people back then would understand—and perhaps it also made for a good story.

Simply put, I don't believe the creation story of Genesis 1:1-2:3 is a lesson in astronomy, physics, or biology. However, if you disagree with me about this, that is fine. You are entitled to draw your own conclusions and have your own opinion. I hope we can at least agree on this much—whatever else the creation story is, it is a lesson in God. And the lesson it teaches is that God created everything, and everything he created was good.

Then we humans messed it up.

Now why does God create mankind in Genesis 1:26-27, and then create them again in Genesis 2? Well, one possibility is that the story of Adam and Eve is not history but allegory or parable, intended to explain how we humans rebelled against God by wanting to be "like God," as we saw with Adam and Eve.

But if you prefer a more literal approach, try this. Genesis 2:7 says that God formed a man from the dust and breathed into him the breath of life, and the man became a living "soul." Under this interpretation, Adam and Eve were not the first humans, but they *were* the first humans to possess a soul. And perhaps those earlier humans were the ones who mated with the sons of Adam and Eve later.[6]

Questions to ponder or discuss: Genesis 1:26 says that God made mankind "in Our image"—which refers to God's *spiritual* image. What does it mean to be made in the spiritual image of God? How are humans similar to God? How are we different from him?

---

6. One possible problem with this interpretation is Genesis 1:26, which says that God made man "in Our image"—which refers to God's *spiritual* image. To me, Genesis 1:26 seems pretty meaningless unless those men and women possessed an eternal soul. Personally, I have trouble accepting the story of Adam and Eve as historical. I believe it is more like a parable. But if you believe Adam and Eve were real, historical persons, that's fine, too. The people who know the truth are long gone.

Chapter 3
Cain and Abel
(Genesis 4:1–16)

Genesis chapter four presents us with the first murder in the Bible, when Cain kills his brother Abel. The source of Cain's animosity was apparently jealousy over the Lord's acceptance of Abel's offering and rejection of Cain's offering. Abel, who was a shepherd, offered a sacrifice from "the firstlings of his flock," whereas Cain, a farmer, gave an offering "from the fruit of the ground."[7]

Genesis doesn't tell us the reason Cain's offering was rejected. Perhaps Abel gave the best he had and Cain did not. Or maybe the key is found in Leviticus 17:11[8] and Hebrews 9:22,[9] which tell us that the shedding of blood is necessary for atonement and forgiveness. Or perhaps both are true.

But I believe the real difference was the respective attitudes of Abel and Cain. Hebrews 11:4 says: "By faith Abel offered to God a better sacrifice than Cain, through which he obtained the testimony that he was righteous." Abel made his offering with faith and humility. Cain did not.

Cain's attitude becomes apparent in what happened next. When God rejected his offering, Cain became "very

---

7. Genesis 4:3-4

8. Leviticus 17:11 says [the Lord speaking to Moses]: "For the life of the flesh is in the blood, and I have given it to you on the altar to make atonement for your souls; for it is the blood by reason of the life that makes atonement."

9. Hebrews 9:22: "And according to the Law, *one may* almost *say*, all things are cleansed with blood, and without shedding of blood there is no forgiveness."

angry and his countenance fell."[10] Although the Lord warned him not to cultivate this anger, for "sin is crouching at the door,"[11] Cain did not listen, resulting in Abel's murder. Then after the murder, instead of repenting, Cain lied when God confronted him. And when God punished him, Cain threw a pity party for himself.

Even as Cain was making his offering, God could see the evil lurking in his heart. As 1 Samuel 16:7 says, "God sees not as man sees, for man looks at the outward appearance, but the LORD looks at the heart."

A gift given with the wrong attitude cannot please God. Paul tells us that in 1 Corinthians 13:3: "And if I give all my possessions to feed the poor . . . but do not have love, it profits me nothing." Micah 6:7-8 says that God values justice, kindness, and humility far more than "thousands of rams." And in Matthew 5:23-24 Jesus seems to say that resolving a dispute with a friend is more important than any offering.

Cain's heart was not right with God, and I believe that is why his offering was rejected. The evil lurking in his heart led to murder—and punishment.

Questions to ponder or discuss: Which is more important—the amount of the gift or the attitude of the giver? Explain. What attitude should we have when we give to God? (For starters, see 2 Corinthians 9:7.[12])

---

10. Genesis 4:5

11. Genesis 4:7

12. 2 Corinthians 9:7: "Each one *must* do just as he has purposed in his heart, not grudgingly or under compulsion, for God loves a cheerful giver."

Chapter 4
The "Sons of God" and the Nephilim
(Genesis 6:1–4)

Genesis 6:1-4 contains the strange story of the "sons of God" mating with the "daughters of men." Who were these "sons of God"?

Two explanations seem possible. One is that they were angelic beings, as in Job 1:6[13] and Job 38:7.[14] If so, then they were surely fallen angels—i.e., demons. Those who object to this interpretation point out that angels and demons are spiritual beings, and therefore they could not have mated with human women. But if that objection is valid, then how did the Incarnation of Christ come about? Mary, the mother of Jesus, was a young woman, while God is most certainly a spiritual being.

The other explanation is that "sons of God" refers to humans who are faithful to God, as in John 1:12[15] and Romans 8:14.[16] Thus, the "sons of God" in Genesis 6 were descendants of Enosh who "began to call upon the name of the LORD."[17] When they mated with the daughters of idolatrous

---

13. Job 1:6: "Now there was a day when the sons of God came to present themselves before the LORD, and Satan also came among them."

14. Job 38:7:

> When the morning stars sang together
> And all the sons of God shouted for joy?

15. John 1:12: "But as many as received Him, to them He gave the right to become children of God, *even* to those who believe in His name."

16. Romans 8:14: "For all who are being led by the Spirit of God, these are sons of God."

17. Genesis 4:26

men, they were corrupted—leading God to regret having made mankind at all.

Genesis 6:4 says that this happened when the "Nephilim" were on the earth. The Nephilim are also mentioned in Numbers 13:33, as part of the story of the twelve Israelites who went to spy on Canaan.[18] When the spies returned, ten of them brought back a dire warning about the people of the land: "we saw the Nephilim . . . and we became like grasshoppers in our own sight, and so we were in their sight." This verse adds that "the sons of Anak are part of the Nephilim." These sons of Anak—the Anakim—also appear in Deuteronomy 2:10-11[19] and 2:21,[20] where we learn that the former inhabitants of Moab and Ammon were "a people as great, numerous, and tall as the Anakim."

So the Nephilim, and their cousins the Anakim, were apparently tall, powerful, intimidating people—perhaps not unlike the large and menacing Goliath (although the Bible does not say that Goliath was a descendant of the Nephilim or the Anakim).

If you believe that a literal worldwide flood destroyed all of mankind except for Noah and his family members (Genesis 6-8), then the Nephilim of Numbers 13 cannot be the descendants of those in Genesis 6, since the latter would have drowned in that flood. In that case, perhaps "Nephilim" became a generic term for people of large or tall proportions.

---

18. Canaan refers to Palestine, which is modern Israel.

19. Deuteronomy 2:10-11: "The Emim lived there formerly, a people as great, numerous, and tall as the Anakim."

20. Deuteronomy 2:21: " . . . a people as great, numerous, and tall as the Anakim, but the LORD destroyed them before them. And they dispossessed them and settled in their place. . . ."

Chapter 4 – The "Sons of God" and the Nephilim

Questions to ponder or discuss: Moses warned the Israelites not to intermarry with non-Israelites in the Promised Land, lest they be led into idolatry. [21] Joshua gave a similar warning.[22] These warnings proved to be accurate.[23] Even King Solomon was led into idolatry by his foreign wives. Why do you think idolatry and evil resulted from such marriages? What problems do Christians risk when they marry unbelievers? What do you think of Paul's advice (which he concedes is *not* from God) for the Christian who has an unbelieving spouse?[24]

---

21. Deuteronomy 7:3-4: "Furthermore, you shall not intermarry with them. . . . For they will turn your sons away from following Me to serve other gods; then the anger of the LORD will be kindled against you and He will quickly destroy you."

22. Joshua 23:12-13: "For if you ever go back and cling to the rest of these nations, these which remain among you, and intermarry with them, so that you associate with them and they with you, know with certainty that the LORD your God will not continue to drive these nations out from before you; but they will be a snare and a trap to you, and a whip on your sides and thorns in your eyes, until you perish from off this good land which the LORD your God has given you."

23. See for example, Judges 3:5-7: "The sons of Israel lived among the Canaanites, the Hittites, the Amorites, the Perizzites, the Hivites, and the Jebusites; and they took their daughters for themselves as wives, and gave their own daughters to their sons, and served their gods. The sons of Israel did what was evil in the sight of the LORD, and forgot the LORD their God and served the Baals and the Asheroth."

24. 1 Corinthians 7:12-13 and 7:15 says: "But to the rest I say, not the Lord, that if any brother has a wife who is an unbeliever, and she consents to live with him, he must not divorce her. And a woman who has an unbelieving husband, and he consents to live with her, she must not send her husband away. . . . Yet if the unbelieving one leaves, let him leave; the brother or the sister is not under bondage in such cases, but God has called us to peace."

Chapter 5
Noah and the Flood
(Genesis 6:5 – 8:19)

I cannot tell you whether the story of Noah and the flood is history, hyperbole, legend, parable, or fantasy. To my knowledge, scientists have not found any evidence of a worldwide flood. However, the flood story is part of so many ancient cultures that I have trouble dismissing it as complete fiction. In any event, we can learn a lot from the story, whether it is fact, fiction, or somewhere in between.

First, we see that God will not tolerate evil indefinitely. When we consider his omniscience, we can easily understand why. He doesn't merely see our cruelty to one another—he *experiences* it, just as we do. He feels each blow and suffers our pain as much as we do. No wonder he longs for a world where love and kindness prevail.

Second, he will go out of his way to preserve goodness in the world. Thus, he delayed his judgment to give Noah time to build a huge boat[25] to save himself and his family.

Third, God is merciful, for he preserves not only the righteous Noah and his wife, but also his sons, Shem, Ham, and Japheth, and their wives. The Lord also provided food for them to eat, for although Noah took only one pair of most animals, God instructed him to take *seven* pairs of the "clean" animals—i.e., animals that Noah and his family could lawfully kill and eat.[26]

---

25. Genesis 6:15 tells us that God instructed Noah to build a boat that was 300 cubits long, fifty cubits wide, and thirty cubits high. A cubit was equivalent to approximately eighteen inches, or one and one-half feet, so Noah's boat would have measured about 450' x 75' x 45'.

26. Genesis 7:2; see also Leviticus 11:1-31

You may well ask, "Where is God's mercy toward those who perished?" We will revisit this question when we talk about Israel's victories over the Amorites and the Canaanites. But for now, consider 1 Peter 4:6, which tells us that after Jesus died on the cross he preached to those who are dead "that though they are judged in the flesh as men, they may live in the spirit according to *the will of* God." Those who perished in the flood lost their lives on earth, but they can still receive eternal life if they listen to Jesus in the next life.

And that is another key to understanding the Old Testament—what I call The Eternal Perspective. This life is simply unimportant compared to eternity—and eternity is where God wants us to be.

Questions to ponder or discuss: C.S. Lewis[27] believed that God is outside of time, meaning that for him the "future" is as real as the past and present are to us. Thus, Lewis argues, when Jesus preached to the dead he spoke not only to those who had died before Jesus' time, but also to those who died after that—including those who have passed away in our own lifetimes.

What do you think of that line of reasoning? If we get a second chance at eternal life in the hereafter, does that mean we can live our lives now any way we please? (Hint: Read chapter six of Romans.)

---

27. Clive Staples Lewis (1898 – 1963)—better known as C.S. Lewis, or "Jack" to his friends—was an Oxford teacher, a Cambridge professor, and a Christian writer and apologist. Among his most famous writings are: *Pilgrim's Regress, The Problem of Pain, The Screwtape Letters, Mere Christianity*, and seven children's books entitled *The Chronicles of Narnia*.

Chapter 6
The Tower of Babel
(Genesis 11:1 – 9)

Ever since Adam and Eve, pride has been our biggest problem. I am *not* talking about pride in the sense of positive self-esteem, justified confidence in one's own abilities, or the satisfaction of a job well done. I mean the haughty pride that makes us think we are self-sufficient, and that revels in human accomplishments, all while ignoring the inevitability of death and decay.

I'm talking about the arrogance that tells us we don't need God—or worse, that we can "be like God." (See Adam and Eve.) That is what Genesis 11:1-9 is about.

Men tried to build a tower "in the land of Shinar"[28] that would reach "into heaven." It was to be a structure so grand that it would "make for ourselves a name."[29] The Tower of Babel was all about pride. Its sole purpose was to demonstrate the greatness of mankind. That is a recipe for disaster, because that kind of pride pulls us away from God by fooling us into thinking he is irrelevant.

God frustrated their plan by confusing their speech—that is, giving them different languages—and scattering them on the face of the earth. He didn't do this to be cruel or malicious, but to check their pride. He did it to show them their own limitations.

When we see our own fragility, we often realize that we need God after all. The famous saying, "There are no

---

28. As the name "Babel" implies, Shinar refers to Babylonia. See Daniel 1:1-2, which says Nebuchadnezzar king of Babylon brought the king of Judah and some items from the temple "to the land of Shinar."

29. Genesis 11:4

atheists in a foxhole," is an illustration of this. When a soldier faces possible imminent death on the battlefield, he is likely to seek God.

We are often closest to God when we are at our weakest.

Questions to ponder or discuss: Paul talks about weakness in 2 Corinthians 12:9-10.[30] What do you think Paul would say about the importance of our scientific and technological progress—for example, in medicine, agriculture, business, space exploration, etc.? How, if at all, has that progress enhanced our arrogance about human achievements? Has that progress given us a false sense of human invulnerability? Why or why not?

---

30. 2 Corinthians 12:9-10 says:

> And He has said to me, "My grace is sufficient for you, for power is perfected in weakness." Most gladly, therefore, I will rather boast about my weaknesses, so that the power of Christ may dwell in me. Therefore, I am well content with weaknesses, with insults, with distresses, with persecutions, with difficulties, for Christ's sake; for when I am weak, then I am strong.

Chapter 7
God's Covenant With Abram/Abraham
(Genesis 11:26 –13:18 and 17:1-21)

Abram's family originally came from Ur, which was located on the Euphrates River in what is now southern Iraq. After Abram had become an adult, his father Terah moved the family upriver to Haran, in what is now southern Turkey. At that time the family included Abram's wife, Sarai, and his nephew, Lot. Genesis 11:31 tells us that Terah had intended to go to Canaan—which is now the country of Israel—but stopped and settled in Haran.

When Abram was seventy-five years old, the Lord told him to leave Haran and go to a land God would show him. This meant leaving everything and everyone familiar to him. Abram did not hesitate. Genesis 12:4 says, "So Abram went forth as the LORD had spoken to him." Taking Sarai and Lot with him, Abram traveled to Canaan, a distance of more than 500 miles.[31]

Because of his faithful obedience, God made Abram a remarkable promise:

I will make you a great nation,
And I will bless you,
And make your name great;
And I will bless those who bless you,

---

31. Abram and Lot later agreed to separate when their livestock multiplied to the point that the land could no longer support both of them. Abram graciously allowed Lot to choose the land he desired. He went east toward the Jordan River valley, where water was plentiful, settling in Sodom. Abram went west into Canaan, settling in Hebron. See Genesis 13:1-18. Hebron is west of the Dead Sea and about twenty miles south of the city of Jerusalem.

And the one who curses you I will curse.
And in you all the families of the earth will be
blessed.

—Genesis 12:2-3

The promise was all the more remarkable because
Abram and Sarai had no children at the time, and Sarai's
womb appeared to be barren. Yet God promised to give the
land of Canaan to Abram's descendants.

Later God made a covenant with Abram, promising
to make him "the father of a multitude of nations" if he
would be righteous and faithful to God.[32] Furthermore, the
Lord promised to do so through a son who would be born
to Abram and Sarai, whom God renamed Abraham and Sarah. Sure enough, Sarah gave birth to Isaac when she was
ninety years old and Abraham was one-hundred. As a sign
of this covenant, all of Abraham's male descendants were
to be circumcised.

God's covenant with Abraham and his descendants
would later be renewed with Isaac[33] and Jacob,[34] as well as
with their descendants at Mount Sinai.[35]

Questions to ponder or discuss: Abraham's descendants would prove much less faithful to God than was their
patriarch. Why do you think God did not renounce the covenant when this happened? What does this tell us about
whether or not we can rely on God's promises?

---

32. Genesis 17:1-4

33. Genesis 26:1-5

34. Genesis 28:13-15

35. Exodus 19:1-8

Chapter 8
Sodom and Gomorrah
(Genesis chapters 18 – 19)

I have heard the story of Sodom and Gomorrah cited many times by people who claim that it proves that God hates homosexuals, or at least that he hates homosexual conduct. The argument is a poor one, because that is not what this story is really about.[36]

The Middle East has a strong and enduring tradition of hospitality toward strangers and travelers. Genesis 18-19 contrasts the wickedness of the people of Sodom with Abraham's righteousness by showing how differently they treated three Heavenly visitors (two angels and the Lord) who were disguised as men.

Abraham rolled out the red carpet, inviting them to rest and wash their feet while he and Sarah prepared a small feast. In contrast, only Abraham's nephew, Lot, gave the two angels a similar welcome when they reached Sodom. Soon thereafter the men of Sodom descended on Lot's house, demanding that the two visitors be handed over "that we may have [sexual] relations with them." As in the days of Noah, God felt that he must eradicate such shocking evil.

The extent of the evil in Sodom and Gomorrah is shown in chapter eighteen, for there the Lord agreed, at Abraham's urging, to spare the cities if even ten righteous people could be found there. But the Lord could not find ten, and the cities were destroyed. Only Lot and his family

---

36. Those people would do better to cite Leviticus 18:22, Leviticus 20:13, Romans 1:26-27, 1 Corinthians 6:9, and 1 Timothy 1:10. But that's another subject.

escaped—all except Lot's wife, for she disobeyed the angels' instructions and paid for it with her life.

Lot would become the father of the Moabites and the Ammonites,[37] people who lived east of the Dead Sea. We will meet them again after the Exodus.

Questions to ponder or discuss: Like Lot's wife, people in the Old Testament frequently suffered severely when they disobeyed God or his representatives. Do you believe God still punishes people for disobedience? Why or why not? (Compare John 9:1-3 and Hebrews 12:7.[38])

---

37. After the destruction of Sodom and Gomorrah, Lot and his two daughters withdrew to a cave in the mountains. The daughters, fearing that this isolation would prevent them from marrying and having children, got their father drunk and each had sexual intercourse with him. As a result, they both became pregnant. The older daughter gave birth to Moab, who became the ancestor of the Moabites. The younger daughter also had a son, whom she named Ben-ammi, the father of the Ammonites. See Genesis 19:30-38.

38. John 9:1-3: "As He [Jesus] passed by, He saw a man blind from birth. And His disciples asked Him, 'Rabbi, who sinned, this man or his parents, that he would be born blind?' Jesus answered, '*It was* neither *that* this man sinned, nor his parents, but *it was* so that the works of God might be displayed in him.' "

Hebrews 12:7: "It is for discipline that you endure; God deals with you as with sons; for what son is there whom *his* father does not discipline?"

Chapter 9
Abraham and Isaac
(Genesis 22:1 – 22:19)

Could you kill your own child? Would God ever ask you to?

Let's be clear about something before we talk about Genesis 22. The Law that God would give to Moses several hundred years later absolutely prohibited human sacrifice.[39] So I am confident God had no intention of allowing Isaac to die when he commanded Abraham to "Take now your son, your only son, whom you love, Isaac, and go to the land of Moriah,[40] and offer him there as a burnt offering on one of the mountains of which I will tell you."[41] But of course Abraham didn't know that.

The language God used is enlightening. He reminds Abraham that Isaac is not only his son, but his "only son, whom you love." God seems to deliberately make it hard for Abraham to obey. Furthermore, Isaac was the son through whom all of God's promises to Abraham were to be fulfilled.[42]

God demands to be first in our lives—more important than spouse or children or any possessions. Remember what Jesus said in Matthew 10:37—if you love parents or children more than him, you are not worthy of him. The foremost commandment is to love God with all your heart,

---

39. See Leviticus 18:21, Leviticus 20:2-5, and Deuteronomy 18:9-10.

40. Mount Moriah would become the site of Solomon's temple. See 2 Chronicles 3:1.

41. Genesis 22:2

42. Genesis 17:19-21

soul, and mind.[43] Family is important, but God has to be *more* important.

So the Lord set up a real-life test of Abraham's faith and devotion by forcing him to choose between God and his only son.

People have speculated that Abraham had faith that God would resurrect Isaac's lifeless body if Abraham killed him. I don't know if that's true or not, but one thing is clear—Abraham trusted God enough to do as he was told regardless of the consequences. Unlike so many others in the Old Testament, Abraham passed his test of faith with flying colors.

Of course, God's angel stopped Abraham before he slew Isaac, and provided a ram to sacrifice in his place.

Questions to ponder or discuss: Difficult times can test our faith. How has your faith in God been tested? And how did you do? How can you do better in the future?

---

43. Matthew 22:36-38

Chapter 10
Isaac and Rebekah
(Genesis chapter 24)

One thing I love about the Bible—and particularly the Old Testament—is how real and human the characters are. In Genesis 24 we are introduced to two people who will play critical future roles: Rebekah and Laban.

First we meet the beautiful, kind, and plucky Rebekah. She was the granddaughter of Abraham's brother, Nahor. Sometime after Sarah's death,[44] Abraham sent his servant back to Haran, in southern Turkey, where Abraham's father had settled.[45] The servant's mission was to find a wife for Isaac, who by then was about thirty-seven years old.[46]

As the servant neared his destination, he asked God for a sign: that the woman who was to be Isaac's wife would not only give the servant a drink of water, but would also offer to draw water for his camels. Rebekah did so. The servant immediately responded by giving her expensive gifts—a gold nose ring and two gold bracelets.

When Rebekah later learned that God had arranged a marriage for her to the son of her very wealthy great uncle, Abraham, she was ready to set out on the long journey immediately. Like Abraham, Rebekah displayed great faith and obedience to the will of God by leaving everything and everyone she knew at God's command.

---

44. Genesis 23:1-2 tells us that Sarah died in Hebron at age 127.

45. See Genesis 11:31, 24:2-9, and 27:43.

46. Compare Genesis 23:1-2 and Genesis 17:15-17. See also Genesis 25:20, which says Isaac was forty years old when he married Rebekah.

The other person we meet is Rebekah's brother, Laban. He at least honored and respected God, for he and his father, Bethuel, obediently consented to God's plan for Rebekah. But Genesis 24:30 hints at Laban's mercenary nature when it says that he ran to meet Abraham's servant "when he saw the ring and the bracelets on his sister's wrists." Laban's greed would be on full display in his future dealings with Rebekah's son, Jacob.

So it was that Rebekah journeyed to Canaan with Abraham's servant and became Isaac's wife. Genesis 24:67 tells us that he loved Rebekah—a cousin he had never met—and that their marriage provided comfort for him after Sarah's death.

Question to ponder or discuss: The Greatest Commandment is to love God with all our heart, soul, and mind (Matthew 22:36-38). So why does God seem to emphasize faith and obedience, rather than love, in Genesis?

Chapter 11
Jacob and Esau
(Genesis 25:19 – 25:34 and 27:1 – 28:5)

Were two brothers ever more different than Jacob and Esau? The first-born Esau grew up to be a hunter, "a man of the field,"[47] and apparently very simple-minded. His brother Jacob became a "peaceful" man who lived in tents, but also a schemer.[48]

We see the contrast immediately in Genesis 25:29-34. Jacob cooked some lentil stew, and Esau came in from the field hungry. In return for a bowl of stew and some bread, he sold his birthright to Jacob. This was no trivial asset Esau so casually discarded, for the first-born son was entitled to twice the inheritance of other male children.[49] In addition, the first-born son was entitled to greater honor, and presumably the covenant blessings God had promised to Abraham and his descendants. Thus, the author of Genesis criticizes Esau for despising his birthright.

When he was forty years old, Esau married two Hittite women against his parents' wishes, which "brought grief" to them, for they probably wanted him to marry within the family as Isaac had done.[50]

We see the craftiness of Jacob and his mother, Rebekah, when they conspired to deprive Esau of his father's blessing by having Jacob pretend to be Esau. The idea was Rebekah's, but Jacob went along. And their plan worked.

---

47. Genesis 25:27

48. Genesis 25:27

49. See Deuteronomy 21:15-17.

50. Genesis 26:34

Isaac, who was old and nearly blind, blessed Jacob instead of Esau. The blessing included a pronouncement that Jacob be "master of your brothers" and that "your mother's sons bow down to you."[51]

When Esau learned what had happened, he vowed to kill his brother. So Rebekah arranged for Isaac to send Jacob to Haran,[52] to her brother Laban, where she knew her younger son would be safe. Twenty years later Jacob and Esau would be reunited, and all would be forgiven.[53] Esau, also known as Edom, would become the father of the Edomites[54]—whom we will meet again after the Exodus. The descendants of Jacob—whom God would later rename Israel[55]—would become the Israelites.

Question to ponder or discuss: In his younger days, Jacob aggressively went after what he wanted, rather than waiting on God to bless him. Why is it often hard for us to wait for God's blessings?

---

51. Genesis 27:29

52. Haran may be another name for Paddan-aram, which is mentioned in Genesis 25:20, 28:2, 28:5-7, 31:18, 33:18, 35:9, 35:26, and 46:15. See also Genesis 48:7, which refers to "Paddan." Or Paddan-aram may have been the region in which Haran was situated.

53. See Genesis 33:4-16.

54. Genesis 36:9; see also Genesis 25:30

55. Genesis 35:10

Chapter 12
Jacob and Laban
(Genesis 28:10 – 29:30 and 30:25 – 31:16)

After stealing his brother's blessing, Jacob journeyed to Haran, to the family of his mother Rebekah. There he went to work for his uncle, Laban, Rebekah's brother.

Jacob fell in love with Laban's younger daughter, Rachel, so he agreed to work for his uncle for seven years in return for her hand in marriage. But at the end of the seven years, Laban substituted his older daughter, Leah, as Jacob's bride. Jacob did not learn of the deceit until after the marriage had been consummated.

We may wonder how Jacob remained so ignorant of his new wife's identity. There are at least two possibilities. One is that the wedding festivities made him too drunk to recognize the substitution. The other possibility is that Leah wore her veil until after the wedding night, which was the custom then. Or perhaps it was a combination of the two.

In any event, Laban insisted on seven more years of labor for Rachel, and Jacob agreed. However, contrary to what I thought when I was a boy, he did not have to wait another seven years to marry Rachel. He was instead able to marry her only a week after his marriage to Leah, even though he still owed Laban another seven years of labor for Rachel's hand.

Laban's deceitfulness would soon backfire on him, for Jacob was a clever adversary. At the end of the second seven-year period, the two of them made a bargain: Jacob would continue to work for his uncle in return for all of the black sheep and the speckled and spotted goats—in other words, the less desirable animals. Laban would keep the rest. In this way Jacob's honesty would be unquestionable, for the color of the animals would conclusively establish to whom they belonged.

This seemed like a good deal for Laban, until Jacob engineered the herds to produce mostly black sheep and speckled and spotted goats.[56] Furthermore, he ensured that the healthiest animals were those in his own flocks. Thus, during the six years that Jacob continued to work for his uncle, he became wealthy at Laban's expense. This produced discord between Jacob and Laban's family. After about twenty years in Haran, an angel of the Lord appeared to Jacob in a dream and told him to return home to Canaan.

Questions to ponder or discuss: Along Jacob's journey to Haran, Genesis 28:11-15 tells us that he had a dream in which angels were ascending and descending a ladder that reached to heaven, after which the Lord appeared and promised to multiply Jacob's descendants "like the dust of the earth," to give them the land where Jacob was lying, and to protect Jacob and bring him back to this land one day. When Jacob awoke, he said, "Surely the LORD is in this place, and I did not know it."[57] What are some places where we might fail to see the Lord's presence? Have there been times when you failed to see the Lord's presence in your life?

---

56. Genesis 30:37-42 tells us that Jacob used striped rods to induce the mating animals to produce discolored offspring. But many suspect Jacob also possessed at least a rudimentary knowledge of how genetics works—that is, the importance of dominant and recessive characteristics.

57. Genesis 28:16

Chapter 13
Jacob's Twelve Sons
(Genesis 29:31 – 30:24 and 35:16 – 35:20)

Jacob had twelve sons by his two wives, Rachel and Leah, and their two handmaidens, Bilhah and Zilpah.

Jacob's prolificacy was primarily due to the rivalry between his two wives, Rachel and Leah. Like Sarah and Rebekah before her, Rachel had trouble conceiving children. Leah, on the other hand, was very fertile and gave Jacob four sons in quick succession—Reuben, Simeon, Levi, and Judah.

A woman's worth in those days was frequently measured by how many children she could bear—because children meant unpaid farm workers, security in a parent's old age, and a legacy to carry on after a parent's death. Being barren made a woman a second class citizen—a person to be scorned or pitied by other women. So in desperation Rachel allowed Jacob to conceive children through her maid, Bilhah, who gave birth to Dan and Naphtali—sons whom Rachel could claim and raise as her own.

Leah, now past childbearing age but not to be outdone, offered her own maid to Jacob. That maid, Zilpah, gave Jacob two more sons, Gad and Asher. After this, Leah miraculously had two more sons of her own: Issachar and Zebulun.

Finally, after many years of being Jacob's favorite wife but unable to give him children, Rachel became pregnant with Joseph, and later Benjamin. Sadly, Rachel died while giving birth to Benjamin.

With one qualification, these twelve sons became the twelve tribes of Israel. The qualification was that Joseph's two sons, Ephraim and Manasseh, were each treated as a separate tribe—in other words, as if they too were sons of

Jacob. So really, the "twelve tribes" were thirteen in number.

Questions to ponder or discuss: In the developed world today, including the United States, children are often more of a financial burden than an economic asset. Yet most couples rejoice over each new birth, and those who are unable to conceive often turn to fertility drugs, surrogates, or adoption in an effort to have children. Do you think this desire for children is due to genetics, instinct, culture, a combination of these, or something else? How do verses like Genesis 1:28[58] and Genesis 9:1[59] impact your answer?

---

58. Genesis 1:28: "God blessed them; and God said to them, 'Be fruitful and multiply, and fill the earth, and subdue it; and rule over the fish of the sea and over the birds of the sky and over every living thing that moves on the earth.' "

59. Genesis 9:1: "And God blessed Noah and his sons and said to them, 'Be fruitful and multiply, and fill the earth.' "

Chapter 14
Jacob Returns to Canaan
(Genesis chapters 32 – 33)

I served twelve years on active duty in the Navy, but in 1991 I felt very strongly that God wanted me to leave the active service. So I submitted my resignation. Never before had I felt more strongly that I was in God's will. Then months went by without a job, and my faith waivered. I wondered if I had misread God and mistaken my own feelings for his leading. So I can sympathize with poor Jacob in Genesis 32.

The chapter opens by telling us that the angels of God met Jacob at a place he named Mahanaim, which means "two camps" — that is, his and God's. He must have been feeling very confident that God was with him at that point. Then he sent messengers with a friendly greeting to his brother Esau. The envoys returned with what seemed like an ominous warning: Esau, the brother Jacob had cheated out of his birthright and his blessing, "is coming to meet you, and four hundred men are with him."[60]

Jacob's faith waivered. Rather than trusting God, he went back to his old scheming ways. He divided his family and his wealth so that if Esau attacked one group, the other might escape. He also prayed for deliverance. But I do not believe he had yet learned to fully trust God, because he sent lavish gifts of livestock to Esau, hoping to win his favor and appease his anger. Jacob was still relying on himself instead of God.

Finally, he sent his wives, children, and possessions across the Jabbok River and was left alone with God.

---

60. Genesis 32:6

Hosea 12:4 tells us that Jacob wrestled with an angel that night. Genesis 32:24 says he wrestled with a "man." Personally, I think his strongest opponents that night were his doubts and his fear. In any event, by daybreak he had learned to put all of his faith in God.

As a result of his struggles that night, Jacob received a permanent limp from a dislocated hip, and a new name: Israel, which means "he who strives with God," or "God strives." It can also mean, "he who perseveres." Jacob struggled with God in the sense that he fought to vanquish his unbelief, and prevailed by placing his trust in God.

In the end things worked out well for him. Esau gave him a warm welcome, and the two brothers were reunited. Jacob settled near Shechem.[61]

Things worked out for me, too, by the way. Unable to get a job, I opened a private law practice and God opened doors for me that I never knew existed. And I was close to home when my aging parents needed me most.

Question to ponder or discuss: Think about the times in your life when you have felt abandoned by God. What do you think God was trying to teach you during those times?

---

61. Shechem was a city in central Canaan, north of Jerusalem.

Chapter 15
Leah's Children
(Genesis 34:1 – 35:4, 35:22, and 38:1 – 38:26)

The odds are that Jacob had many daughters in addition to his twelve sons. But only one daughter is mentioned in Genesis—Dinah, daughter of Leah—perhaps because she plays a role in an ugly incident involving Jacob's sons.

Dinah attracted the attention of Shechem, a Hivite prince, who raped her and then asked for her hand in marriage. Jacob's outraged sons pretended to agree to the arrangement, but only on the condition that the males in the city be circumcised. Enticed by Jacob's wealth, the men agreed. But when they were in pain from the circumcision, Simeon and Levi led an attack upon the city, killing the men, capturing their families, and stealing their possessions.

The actions of Simeon and Levi were completely without God's authority or approval. Indeed, Genesis 35:2-4 hints that Jacob's family members had adopted the idolatry of the Canaanites, which may give us a clue as to why they had become capable of such wicked behavior.

Jacob apparently knew nothing of his sons' plan until after it had been carried out. He was understandably angry about the violence, and worried that the other inhabitants of Canaan would unite and attack. Perhaps to avoid that problem, God sent Jacob and his family to Bethel.

There Jacob's first-born son, Reuben, seduced Bilhah, Rachel's maid, who was the mother of Reuben's half-brothers, Dan and Naphtali. Because of this, Reuben lost the preeminence ordinarily due the first-born son.[62]

_____

62. See Genesis 49:3-4 and 1 Chronicles 5:1.

Chapter 15 – Leah's Children

Judah, the fourth oldest of Jacob's sons, had his own failings. Judah was the father of three sons: Er, Onan, and Shelah. Er married a woman named Tamar, but then was killed by the Lord for his wickedness before he had any children. The Law required Onan to father a child with Tamar on behalf of his deceased brother.[63] But Onan was not enthusiastic about this law, so he resorted to *coitus interruptus* in an effort to avoid conception. As a result, the Lord struck him dead, too. (This incident is sometimes erroneously cited as evidence that masturbation is a sin, but that is not what Onan did.)

Having lost two sons, Judah was reluctant to give his third son, Shelah, as a husband for Tamar for fear of losing him too. So Judah procrastinated. Eventually, Tamar took matters into her own hands. She travelled to meet Judah at the town of Enaim. Disguising herself as a temple prostitute, she had sex with him. Then she accepted his seal, cord, and staff as a pledge against future payment, and went back home. When she began to show in her pregnancy, she provided Judah's seal, cord, and staff as evidence that he was the father, which reminded him that he had not been fair to her. This allowed her to escape punishment for engaging in intercourse with her father-in-law.

Questions to ponder or discuss: These men—Reuben, Simeon, Levi, and Judah—were sons of Leah, the wife Jacob was tricked into marrying. Genesis 29:31 tells us that Leah was "unloved"—literally, "hated"—by Jacob. And we learn in Genesis 37:3-4 that Jacob loved his son, Joseph, more than all of his other brothers. Clearly, Israel was no father of the year. What impact do you think Jacob's attitude and behavior toward his children, and their mother,

---

63. See Deuteronomy 25:5-6. See also chapter forty-two, "The Second Census."

31

may have had in leading his four oldest sons into idolatry, murder, and sexual immorality? How important is a father in his children's lives? How does a husband's love for his wife positively impact their children?

Chapter 16
Joseph
(Genesis 37:2 – 37:36 and chapters 39 – 50)

Have you ever felt that life was unfair? Have you ever questioned God's existence because so much evil and injustice exists in the world—or because something painful happened to you or to someone you care about? Then take a lesson from the life of Joseph. If anyone had a right to be angry at God, Joseph did.

Joseph had a tough life when he was a young man. At about the age of seventeen, his brothers plotted to kill him, but instead sold him into slavery to some Midianite traders, who took him to Egypt. There he was falsely accused of rape and imprisoned because he did the right thing by refusing the advances of the wife of his Egyptian master, Potiphar.

While Joseph was in prison, God enabled him to interpret the dreams of Pharaoh's baker and cupbearer, correctly predicting that the cupbearer would soon be restored to his rightful position and the baker would be executed. But Joseph languished in prison for two more years because the cupbearer, after being reinstated, forgot about poor Joseph.

Because of the wickedness and thoughtlessness of others, he lost twelve to thirteen years of his life to slavery and imprisonment.[64]

---

64. Genesis 37:2 says: "Joseph, when seventeen years of age, was pasturing the flock with his brothers while he was still a youth, along with the sons of Bilhah and the sons of Zilpah, his father's wives, And Joseph brought back a bad report about them to their father." This was one of the grievances Joseph's brothers had against him that soon thereafter led them to sell him into slavery, so Joseph was probably seven-

Yet Joseph bore no ill will toward his brothers or toward God. He recognized that what he had endured had brought him to the place where he was—ruler of Egypt, second only to Pharaoh.[65] Joseph understood that God had placed him there so that he could prepare Egypt for the seven years of famine that would follow seven years of abundance. With twenty-twenty hindsight, Joseph realized that God had a plan all along.

After Jacob's death, Joseph reassured his brothers, who were terrified that he would finally take revenge on them: "Do not be afraid, for am I in God's place? As for you, you meant evil against me, *but* God meant it for good in order to bring about this present result, to preserve many people alive. So therefore, do not be afraid; I will provide for you and your little ones."[66]

Joseph forgave his brothers and took care of them in Egypt during the famine and afterward. As a result, the descendants of Jacob—aka Israel—increased exponentially during the following 400 years that they remained in Egypt.

Question to ponder or discuss: I do not believe that God *sends* terrible things into our lives—such as disease, crime, or natural disasters—but he also doesn't prevent them. Such events may seem unfair to you, or at least diffi-

---

teen or eighteen when he was taken in bondage to Egypt. He got out of prison at age thirty, according to Genesis 41:46: "Now Joseph was thirty years old when he stood before Pharaoh, king of Egypt." This was when Pharaoh "set [Joseph] over all the land of Egypt."(Genesis 41:43) So Joseph was enslaved or imprisoned from about age seventeen, or perhaps eighteen, until age thirty.

65. Joseph received this exalted position after he correctly interpreted Pharaoh's dreams, which foretold seven years of tremendous prosperity followed by seven years of severe famine.

66. Genesis 50:19-21

cult to understand. What are some reasons why God would allow those things to occur?[67]

---

67. I discuss this in chapter three of my book, *Beyond Blind Faith: Reasons For the Hope We Have (1 Peter 3:15)*, which is available on Amazon.com. Chapter three is entitled, "Why Do Bad Things Happen (to Me)?"

Chapter 17
Moses' Early Life
(Exodus chapters 1 – 2)

Exodus 1:8 tells us that "a new king arose over Egypt, who did not know Joseph." That's not surprising, since at least 400 years had passed since the time of Joseph.[68] During that time, the Israelites had become very numerous—600,000 men, not including children, according to Exodus 12:37.[69]

The Egyptians didn't like the Israelites. In the time of Joseph, just eating with an Israelite was considered "loathsome to the Egyptians,"[70] as was the Israelite occupation of shepherd.[71] But now, 400 years later, fear compounded the Egyptians' racial prejudice, for Pharaoh worried that in case of war the Israelites would side with the enemy.

So Pharaoh overworked the Israelites, perhaps hoping many would work themselves to death and thereby decrease the Israelite population. Or maybe he thought they

---

68. We know from the following two verses that the Israelites spent at least four-hundred years in Egypt:

Genesis 15:13: "*God* said to Abram, 'Know for certain that your descendants will be strangers in a land that is not theirs, where they will be enslaved and oppressed four hundred years."(In Acts 7:6, Stephen quotes this verse.)

Exodus 12:40: "Now the time that the sons of Israel lived in Egypt was four hundred and thirty years."

69. The Hebrew could also be translated "600 families," which would be perhaps 50,000 or 60,000 people. However, Numbers 1:20-46, 2:3-32, and 11:21 seem to support the higher number.

70. Genesis 43:32

71. Genesis 46:33-34

would be too tired or too discouraged to procreate. His plan didn't work.

Pharaoh next ordered that all Israelite baby boys be murdered. The baby girls were to be allowed to live, presumably since only the boys were likely to be threats when grown.[72]

Moses was born into this world, the child of two people from the Israelite tribe of Levi. His mother hid him for three months, until he became too big to hide. Then she set him in a basket in the Nile River where she knew the Pharaoh's daughter came to bathe. The plan worked. Pharaoh's daughter found baby Moses and, when he was weaned, raised him as her own.

Moses was educated like a wealthy Egyptian, but he never forgot that he was an Israelite. When he saw an Egyptian beating one of his fellow Hebrews, Moses killed the assailant. Then he fled to Midian, east of the Sinai Peninsula, to avoid Egyptian justice. There he married a Cushite woman named Zipporah and had two sons, Gershom and Eliezer.[73]

In Midian, Moses became a shepherd—until God called him to become one of the greatest Israelite prophets in history.

Question to ponder or discuss: The Egyptian prejudice against shepherds must seem silly to most of us nowadays. What are some of our prejudices that will seem silly to future generations?

_____

72. The girls could of course be used as servants, and perhaps as concubines.

73. See Exodus 2:21-22, 18:2-5, and Numbers 12:1. The Cushites were descendants of Cush, who was a son of Ham and a grandson of Noah, per Genesis 10:1 and 10:6.

Chapter 18
Moses, the Reluctant Prophet
(Exodus 3:1 – 4:23)

The tale of Moses in chapters three and four of Exodus is one of my favorite stories in the Old Testament because I can really sympathize with Moses.

The chapter begins with Moses taking his father-in-law's sheep west into the Sinai Peninsula, all the way to Mount Horeb, which is also known in the Bible as Mount Sinai, "the mountain of God."[74] Although we don't know exactly where Mount Sinai is, most experts believe it to be in the southern portion of the peninsula, about halfway between the Gulf of Suez to the west and the Gulf of Aqaba to the east.

To reach this point, Moses had to travel at least eighty miles, and probably further, which raises the question of why he went so far. Perhaps he was trying to find water or better grazing land for his animals. But whatever Moses' motivation, he was undoubtedly led there by God, even though Moses was not aware of it at the time.

At Mount Sinai he saw an amazing sight—a bush that was on fire, but which was not consumed. Moses must have seen the bush from far away, and his curiosity would have been aroused because the fire didn't go out, nor did it spread. So he turned aside to see it, and there he encountered God, who had a special mission for him: deliver the Israelites from slavery and oppression in Egypt.

---

74. Exodus 3:1

Chapter 18 – Moses, the Reluctant Prophet

Moses felt inadequate to the task, as most of us would in that position. So he tried to excuse himself. But God had an answer for every excuse:

> *Moses*: "Who am I, that I should go to Pharaoh, and that I should bring the sons of Israel out of Egypt?"[75]
>
> *God*: "Certainly I will be with you. . . ."[76]
>
> *Moses*: Whom should I say sent me?
>
> *God*: Tell them, "I AM has sent me to you."[77]
>
> *Moses*: What if they won't believe me?
>
> *God*: Show them these miracles.
>
> *Moses*: But I don't speak well.
>
> *God*: I'll help you.
>
> *Moses*: Couldn't you find someone else?
>
> *God*: Fine. Aaron, your brother, can speak for you.

Now go!

As Moses found out, God doesn't take "no" for an answer. So Moses went to Egypt to confront Pharaoh and demand that he let the Israelites go.

Question to ponder or discuss: God sometimes calls us to do things that are outside of our comfort zone—for example, to assume a leadership position, or talk about our faith with an unbeliever. What does Moses' experience teach us about how we should react in those moments?

---

75. Exodus 3:11

76. Exodus 3:12

77. Exodus 3:14

Chapter 19
The Hardening of Pharaoh's Heart
(Exodus 4:27 - 12:36)

People who wish to put God on trial claim that he was unfair to poor Pharaoh. They point out that God hardened Pharaoh's heart so that he would not allow the Israelites to leave until after God had devastated Egypt with ten plagues. Those ten plagues were:[78]

(1) Nile River turned to blood;
(2) frogs covering the land;
(3) dust turned into gnats;
(4) swarms of insects;
(5) disease that killed livestock;
(6) boils and sores on people and animals;
(7) devastating hail;
(8) devouring locusts;
(9) three days of complete darkness; and
(10) the death of all first-born.

But people who accuse God of injustice miss or ignore several important facts. First, God did not harden Pharaoh's heart until after the sixth plague.[79] Before that, Pharaoh hardened his own heart—in other words, he was stubborn.[80]

Furthermore, Pharaoh took this rigid stance despite the fact that all Moses initially requested was to allow the Israelites to "go a three days' journey into the wilderness

---

78. These ten plagues are discussed in chapters seven through twelve of Exodus.

79. Exodus 9:12

80. See Exodus 7:22, 8:15, 8:19, 8:32, and 9:7.

that we may sacrifice to the LORD our God."[81] Pharaoh was so obstinate and inflexible that he was unwilling to allow the Israelites to be away from their work for even this short period of time. Did Pharaoh suspect that Moses intended to lead the Israelites away and not return? Perhaps, but Exodus does not say so.

Also, God hardened Pharaoh's heart only after Pharaoh had ignored the advice of his own magicians to relent,[82] and only after Pharaoh had twice promised to let the Israelites go and then reneged on that promise.[83]

God gave Pharaoh plenty of opportunities to cooperate, and he repeatedly refused. Only then did God begin to play rough by making Pharaoh even more stubborn than he already was.

But what about Exodus 4:21 and 7:3,[84] in which the Lord tells Moses that he "will harden" Pharaoh's heart so that he will refuse to let the people go? I believe these are simply prophecies about what God would do beginning in Exodus 9:12. The Lord knew Pharaoh's heart better than Pharaoh himself.[85] So the Lord knew that he would not cooperate except under extreme compulsion. In other words, God in his mercy gave Pharaoh chances to do the right thing, but he also knew the man was so arrogant and

---

81. Exodus 5:3

82. Exodus 8:18-19

83. Exodus 8:8-15 and 8:28-32

84. Exodus 4:21: "The LORD said to Moses, 'When you go back to Egypt see that you perform before Pharaoh all the wonders which I have put in your power; but I will harden his heart so that he will not let the people go.' "
Exodus 7:3: "But I will harden Pharaoh's heart that I may multiply My signs and My wonders in the land of Egypt."

85. See Psalm 139:1-4 and Psalm 44:21.

mulish that he would not take advantage of those chances.

Questions to ponder or discuss: To what extent do you believe Pharaoh was free to act contrary to his character? To what extent are you and I free to act contrary to our characters?

Chapter 20
Passover
(Exodus chapter 12)

The Old Testament is primarily about two things, and the first Passover embodies both.

First, God was trying to teach his people to trust him. Passover was perhaps the ultimate test of that trust. God instructed his people to do something that must have sounded crazy at the time: kill a lamb and spread its blood on the doorposts and the lintels of their houses—in other words, on the door frame above and to the side of the door. Those who did so would be safe, but those who disobeyed these instructions would suffer the death of their firstborn child.

God also instructed the people to roast the lamb and eat it that same night, leaving nothing until morning.[86] They would have no leftovers, so they would have to trust God to provide food for them on their journey. They were to eat quickly and be dressed to travel. This allowed them to get underway quickly when Pharaoh gave them their freedom, before Pharaoh changed his mind (which he soon did).

Second, God was trying to teach his people to always put him first, and the Passover lamb is an example of that. The lamb was to be "an unblemished male a year old."[87] "Unblemished" in this context meant that it could not be deformed, defective, diseased, or discolored. It had to be a perfect animal—and thus was among the most valuable animals in the flock. This same requirement would be

---

86. Whatever was left was to be burned, per Exodus 12:10.

87. Exodus 12:5

true of most offerings to the Lord, as we shall see when we get to Mount Sinai. God wants, and demands, our best.

Questions to ponder or discuss: As we have noted before (chapter one), God emphasized trust in the early books of the Old Testament rather than love. How hard is it to love someone you don't trust? How does a lack of trust erode love?

Chapter 21
Crossing the Sea of Reeds
(Exodus chapters 13 – 14)

The shortest route from Egypt to Canaan was along the coast of the Mediterranean Sea, but God did not take the Israelites that way. That was a well-traveled route, with plenty of soldiers and encampments to protect travelers and caravans. God did not want his people to be frightened by the prospect of having to fight their way to Canaan,[88] especially since some of the soldiers in the way were probably Egyptians.

Instead, he led them toward the "Sea of Reeds"[89]—a reference that is now obscure, but which probably refers to one of the lakes or marshes between the Mediterranean Sea and the Gulf of Suez.

Pharaoh saw that the Israelites appeared to be trapped, with water blocking their escape, so he pursued them with his army.

Despite what the Israelites had seen God do for them in Egypt, they lost faith and despaired. This occurred even though they had visual proof of God's presence in their midst, for he was guiding them with a pillar of cloud during the day and a pillar of fire at night.

Moses, however, did not lose faith. He assured the people that God would protect them and deliver them from Pharaoh's army. And that is just what happened—while the pillar of cloud/fire kept the Egyptian army at bay, the waters parted for the Israelites to cross. When Pharaoh's soldiers tried to pursue, the Lord sabotaged their chariot

---

88. Exodus 13:17

89. Exodus 13:18

wheels, bogging them down, then caused the waters to return, drowning them.

Thus the Israelites found themselves in the Sinai Peninsula, free of their Egyptian masters at last. Next stop: Mount Sinai.

Questions to ponder or discuss: Why is it so easy to lose faith when trouble strikes or dangers lurk? When has your faith faltered in a difficult time? How can we avoid such faltering faith in the future?

Chapter 22
The Journey to Mount Sinai
(Exodus 15:22 – 17:7)

After being delivered from Egypt through miracle after miracle, culminating with the parting of the Sea of Reeds and the destruction of Pharaoh's army, the Israelites ought to have had supreme faith in their God and in their leader, Moses. Perhaps they did—until they got thirsty.

The Israelites traveled for three days along the west coast of the Sinai Peninsula, but found no water to drink. Their journey brought them to Marah, where they found water—but it was undrinkable. The people complained, and God showed Moses how to make the water drinkable. After that, the journey continued to the oasis of Elim, where water was plentiful. There the people's faith was renewed—until they got hungry.

Moving on from Elim, the people came to the Wilderness of Sin, where they complained about the lack of food. They reminisced about Egypt, where they had plenty to eat—already forgetting the oppressive conditions there. So God gave them food: quails in the evening and manna in the mornings. (The Sinai Peninsula is along one of the migration routes for quails, which land on the peninsula to rest.)

Exodus 16:31 tells us that the manna tasted like "wafers with honey." This manna was another test of faith— Moses told the people not to save it until the next day,[90] for God would provide more each day. But once again many of them failed the test, and discovered that the manna became rotten overnight. The one exception to this rule revolved

---

90. Exodus 16:19

around the Sabbath, for the people could gather enough manna for two days on the day before the Sabbath and it would stay good both days. Thus, everyone could rest on the Sabbath, and no manna appeared that day.

Now well fed, the faith of the Israelites was re-newed—until they got thirsty again.

God led the people on to Rephidim, where there was no water, and they again complained. Acting on instructions from God, Moses struck a rock, and abundant water flowed out.

Rephidim was probably at or near the base of Mount Sinai, for the rock which Moses struck was "at Horeb."[91] Horeb is another name for Mount Sinai.[92]

Question to ponder or discuss: The Israelites were immature spiritually, so their faith was weak. How do we nourish our faith so that it will grow?[93]

---

91. Exodus 17:6

92. Compare Exodus 19:16-20:20 with Deuteronomy 4:10-14.

93. I discuss this question in chapter one of my book, *Beyond Shallow Faith: Cultivating Christian Maturity (Ephesians 4:13-15)*, entitled, "Spiritual Growth," which is available on Amazon.com.

Chapter 23
The Attack at Rephidim
(Exodus 17:8 – 17:16)

We begin this story in 1 Samuel 15:3, where the Lord commanded Saul, the king of the Israelites, to

> go and strike Amalek and utterly destroy all
> that he has, and do not spare him; but put to
> death both man and woman, child and infant,
> ox and sheep, camel and donkey.

That command has its roots in Exodus 17:8-13, which describes Amalek's attack on the Israelites at Rephidim.

Amalek was a grandson of Esau, Isaac's eldest son and Jacob's brother, so the Amalekites likely were descendants of Isaac and Esau. They lived in southern Canaan and the Negev desert,[94] and probably in the nearby Sinai Peninsula as well. They undoubtedly regarded the Israelites as a threat to their water and food supplies.

Because the Amalekites consistently allied themselves with Israel's enemies, they were a constant thorn in the Israelites' side.[95] That was surely a factor in God's order to Saul, but it was far from the only one.

The Amalekites' attack against the Israelites at Rephidim, as described in Exodus 17:8-13, angered the Lord because it was a cowardly act. Deuteronomy 25:18 explains why. In that verse Moses reminded the Israelites that Amalek "attacked among you all the stragglers at your rear when you were faint and weary." Those stragglers would have consisted primarily of the very old, the very young, the infirm, and perhaps many women. They would not

---

94. See Numbers 13:29, 14:25, and 14:43-45.

95. See, for example, Judges 3:13, 5:14, 6:3, 6:33, 7:12 and 10:12.

49

have been able to keep up with the main body of the Israelites, and could have offered little or no resistance against the Amalekite warriors.

The Amalekites' vile tactics so infuriated the Lord that he ordered the Israelites to "blot out the memory of Amalek from under heaven" once they had conquered the promised land.[96] King Saul would be God's instrument to carry out that order. He failed, by the way, and a remnant of the Amalekites would survive until at least the time of Hezekiah, who was king of Judah from about 728 to 696 B.C.[97]

Amalek's attack at Rephidim failed when Moses sent Joshua to lead a counter-attack. This led to the inspiring story of Aaron and Hur supporting Moses' arms, for the Israelites were victorious in the battle only so long as Moses could keep his arms lifted.

Questions to ponder or discuss: Saul was king of Israel in about the late eleventh century, B.C., which was approximately 250 to 400 years after the time of Moses (depending on when you believe the Exodus occurred). How do you feel about God punishing the Amalekites for the misdeeds of their distant ancestors? Would it affect your answer if you were told that the Amalekites had not changed their ways in the meantime? Do you believe we have people like the Amalekites today? If so, who? And what should God do about them?

---

96. See Exodus 17:14 and Deuteronomy 25:19.

97. See 1 Chronicles 4:41-43.

Chapter 24
The Covenant at Sinai
(Exodus 19:1 – 19:8)

The Israelites reached Mount Sinai about two to three months after leaving Egypt. There God made a covenant with them.

A covenant is a solemn promise. It is similar in some ways to a contract, but more enduring. As in modern American contract law, the covenant in Exodus 19 takes the form of an offer and an acceptance. The offer was made by God in Exodus 19:5-6:

> Now then, if you will indeed obey My voice
> and keep My covenant, then you shall be My
> own possession among all the peoples, for all
> the earth is Mine; and you shall be to Me a
> kingdom of priests and a holy nation.

The people's acceptance is in Exodus 19:8: "All the people answered together and said, 'All that the LORD has spoken we will do!' " The covenant was later renewed before the Israelites entered Canaan.[98]

God promised his people many wonderful things if they performed their part of the covenant by remaining faithful and obedient: peace, victory, prosperity, children, health, long life, and God's presence.[99]

Similarly, he warned them of dire consequences for disobedience, such as disease, defeat, famine, poverty, fear, humiliation, oppression by their enemies, captivity, de-

---

98. Deuteronomy 29:10-29
99. Leviticus 26:3-13

struction, exile, and desolation.[100] Unfortunately, the Israelites were frequently unfaithful and disobedient.

Yet God never disowned them for their disobedience. From his perspective, this covenant was everlasting. No matter how unfaithful the Israelites might be, God would always remain faithful to the covenant: "Yet in spite of this, when they are in the land of their enemies, I will not reject them, nor will I so abhor them as to destroy them, breaking my covenant with them; for I am the LORD their God."[101]

Questions to ponder or discuss: Out of all the peoples on earth, why do you think the Lord chose the Israelites with which to make a covenant? How does 1 Corinthians 1:26-31[102] impact your answer? How do

---

100. Leviticus 26:14-39

101. Leviticus 26:44

102. 1 Corinthians 1:26-31: "For consider your calling, brethren, that there were not many wise according to the flesh, not many mighty, not many noble; but God has chosen the foolish things of the world to shame the wise, and God has chosen the weak things of the world to shame the things which are strong, and the base things of the world and the despised God has chosen, the things that are not, so that He may nullify the things that are, so that no man may boast before God. But by His doing you are in Christ Jesus, who became to us wisdom from God, and righteousness and sanctification, and redemption, so that, just as it is written, 'LET HIM WHO BOASTS, BOAST IN THE LORD.' "

verses like Genesis 15:18[103] and Genesis 22:15-18[104] impact your answer?

In 1 Corinthians 1:26-31, Paul says that in his day God chose people who were foolish, weak, and despised, rather than the wise and the strong. Do you believe God still does that? Why or why not?

---

103. Genesis 15:18: "On that day the LORD made a covenant with Abram, saying, 'To your descendants I have given this land, From the river of Egypt as far as the great river, the river Euphrates.' "

104. Genesis 22:15-18: "Then the angel of the LORD called to Abraham a second time from heaven, and said, 'By Myself I have sworn, declares the LORD, because you have done this thing and have not withheld your son, your only son, indeed I will greatly bless you, and I will greatly multiply your seed as the stars of the heavens and as the sand which is on the seashore; and your seed shall possess the gate of their enemies. In your seed all the nations of the earth shall be blessed, because you have obeyed My voice.' "

Chapter 25
Why God Speaks Through Prophets
(Exodus 19:9 – 19:25, 20:18 – 20:21)

Have you ever wondered why God doesn't make a big show of his existence? The verses which follow the making of the covenant in Exodus 19 provide the answer to that question, while also explaining why God spoke to his people exclusively through prophets.

God told Moses that in three days he would "come down on Mount Sinai in the sight of all the people,"[105] and that he would come in a way "that the people may hear when I speak with you."[106] When the third day arrived, "there were thunder and lightning flashes and a thick cloud upon the mountain and a very loud trumpet sound."[107]

The people were terrified. They "trembled" and "stood at a distance."[108] In fact, they were so frightened that they asked Moses not to let God speak directly to them again, "or we will die."[109]

This reaction of fear is seen throughout the Bible. When people are confronted by the awesome power and majesty of God, they often react just as the Israelites did at Mount Sinai—they are terrified. Moses felt this fear,[110] as did Isaiah[111] and Jesus' disciples.[112]

---

105. Exodus 19:11

106. Exodus 19:9

107. Exodus 19:16

108. Exodus 19:16, 20:18

109. Exodus 20:19

110. Exodus 3:5-6

111. Isaiah 6:5

112. For example, see Matthew 17:5-6, Mark 4:39-41, and Luke 8:35-37.

Chapter 25 – Why God Speaks Through Prophets

When angels appeared to Zacharias, Mary, and the shepherds, the angels had to reassure them by saying, "Do not be afraid."[113]

To get back to the question that opened this chapter, why doesn't God make a big show of his existence? He certainly could do so at any time, as he did at Mount Sinai. But that would only frighten us. It would not achieve what he truly wants from us, which is our trust, our obedience, and our love. Terror like the Israelites felt at the foot of Mount Sinai is counter-productive for God's purposes because it makes us recoil from him rather than draw near.

God granted the Israelites' request that he not speak directly with them again. Thereafter he spoke to the Israelites only through prophets.[114]

Questions to ponder or discuss: If fear is the universal human reaction to the overwhelming power of God, what does this tell us about why God came to us as the man Jesus? Proverbs 1:7 says: "The fear of the LORD is the beginning of knowledge; Fools despise wisdom and instruction." Many modern translations substitute "reverence" for "fear" in this verse. How is reverence different from fear?

---

113. Luke 1:11-13, 1:26-30, and 2:8-10

114. See Deuteronomy 18:15-18: [Moses speaking] "The LORD your God will raise up for you a prophet like me from among you, from your countrymen, you shall listen to him. This is according to all that you asked of the LORD your God in Horeb on the day of the assembly, saying, 'Let me not hear again the voice of the LORD my God, let me not see this great fire anymore, or I will die.' The LORD said to me, 'They have spoken well. I will raise up a prophet from among their countrymen like you, and I will put My words in his mouth, and he shall speak to them all that I command him.' "

Chapter 26
The Ten Commandments
(Exodus 20:1 – 20:17 and chapter 32)

The famous Ten Commandments are set forth in Exodus 20:1-17. Although Exodus 20 doesn't refer to them as "the Ten Commandments," other verses give them that name.[115]

Judaism, Protestantism, and Roman Catholicism disagree about how the commandments in Exodus 20:1-17 should be partitioned to achieve exactly ten. For example, Roman Catholicism labels the prohibition against murder as the fifth commandment, but Judaism and Protestantism label it as number six.

One of the two longest commandments is the prohibition against idolatry in Exodus 20:3-5. God repeatedly emphasized this particular commandment, and warned the Israelites of the dire consequences should they violate it.[116] Nevertheless, idolatry was a constant problem for the Israelites, beginning not long after God gave them the Ten Commandments.

Following God's covenant with the people, Moses went back up on Mount Sinai to receive the Law from the Lord, which took awhile. Exodus 24:18 tells us he was there for forty days and forty nights. The people grew impatient and asked Aaron, Moses' brother, to make a god for them to worship. So Aaron made them a golden calf, which they proclaimed as their god "who brought you up from the land of Egypt."[117]

---

115. See Exodus 34:28, Deuteronomy 4:13, and Deuteronomy 10:4.

116. See for example Deuteronomy 4:25-28 and 8:19-20.

117. Exodus 32:4, 8

Moses and the Lord were understandably upset with the people for doing this. Moses was so angry that he broke the tablets on which "the testimony" (presumably, the Ten Commandments) was written.[118] Then he ground the golden calf into dust, scattered it on the water, and made the Israelites drink it.

Questions to ponder or discuss: In Exodus 32:9-14,[119] God threatens to destroy the Israelites and start over with Moses and his descendants, but Moses appears to talk God out of it. Do you think God truly "changed His mind," as Exodus 32:14 says, or was he merely testing—and perhaps teaching—Moses? Explain.

Do you believe God still tests us today? Why or why not?

---

118. Exodus 32:15-19

119. Exodus 32:9-14:

> The LORD said to Moses, "I have seen this people, and behold, they are an obstinate people. Now then let Me alone, that My anger may burn against them and that I may destroy them; and I will make of you a great nation." Then Moses entreated the LORD his God, and said, "O LORD, why does Your anger burn against Your people whom You have brought out from the land of Egypt with great power and with a mighty hand? Why should the Egyptians speak, saying, 'With evil *intent* He brought them out to kill them in the mountains and to destroy them from the face of the earth'? Turn from Your burning anger and change Your mind about *doing* harm to Your people. Remember Abraham, Isaac, and Israel, Your servants to whom You swore by Yourself, and said to them, 'I will multiply your descendants as the stars of the heavens, and all this land of which I have spoken I will give to your descendants, and they shall inherit *it* forever.'" So the LORD changed His mind about the harm which He said He would do to His people.

Chapter 27
The Tabernacle
(Exodus chapters 25 – 27 and 30)

The Israelites arrived at Mount Sinai in the third month after leaving Egypt,[120] and did not move on from the mountain of God until the second month of the second year after the Exodus.[121] During those eleven months God gave them the Law. He also gave them detailed instructions for constructing the Tabernacle and crafting its furnishings, which they subsequently constructed. The events in the book of Leviticus occurred during those eleven months.

The Israelite people provided all of the materials for the Tabernacle—which included precious metals, colorful cloth, animal skins, costly gems, wood, and more—through voluntary offerings.[122] Skilled craftsmen cut, formed, and fashioned all of the component parts.[123]

The Court of the Tabernacle was approximately one-hundred fifty feet long and seventy-five feet wide.[124] Curtains about seven and one-half feet tall hung around the perimeter of this rectangular Court, presumably to shield it from curious eyes. Inside the Court stood the bronze altar

---

120. Exodus 19:1

121. Numbers 10:11-12

122. See Exodus 25:1-9 and 35:20-29. Indeed, the people were so generous that Moses soon had to stop them from bringing anything further because they had contributed more than enough for the task. See Exodus 36:3-7.

123. Exodus 31:1-11 and 35:30-38:31

124. This would be slightly more than a quarter-acre. It would be almost as large as two-and-a-half basketball courts, or about two-thirds the size of a hockey rink.

for sacrifices, the bronze laver for washing, and the Tent of Meeting.

The Tent of Meeting—or the Tabernacle Tent— measured forty-five feet long, fifteen feet wide, and fifteen feet high. The entrance of the Tent faced east and led to the Holy Place, which occupied two-thirds of the Tent.[125] The Holy Place contained the Table of Showbread,[126] the Lampstand, and the Altar of Incense. All three were overlaid with gold.

The remaining one-third of the Tent constituted the Most Holy Place, or the Holy of Holies. The only entrance to the Holy of Holies was through the Holy Place, and a heavy veil separated the two sections of the Tent. Only the high priest could enter the Holy of Holies, and he could do so only once a year, on the Day of Atonement.[127]

The Holy of Holies contained the Ark of the Covenant, which symbolized God's presence. On top of the Ark sat a heavy lid known as the Mercy Seat. The Ark and the Mercy Seat were both overlaid with gold. According to Hebrews 9:4, the Ark held the "testimony" Moses received from God, a jar with manna, and Aaron's staff which budded.[128] The Ark had rings on each side, through which poles were inserted for the purpose of carrying it—for no one was permitted to actually touch the Ark.[129] The Altar of

---

125. Thus, the Holy Place measured 30' x 15' x 15'. The Most Holy Place occupied the rest of the Tent of Meeting and measured 15' x 15' x 15'.

126. Exodus 25:23-30. The showbread consisted of twelve loaves of bread placed on the golden table in the Tabernacle as an offering to God, and replaced each sabbath. This bread was for the priests to eat. See Leviticus 24:5-9.

127. See Leviticus 16 and Hebrews 9:6-7.

128. See Numbers 17:1-10

129. Exodus 25:12-15 and Numbers 4:15

The Old Testament Made Simple (Part 1)

Incense, the Table of Showbread, and the bronze altar were carried with poles in similar fashion.[130]

All sacrifices had to be offered at "the place which the LORD your God will choose."[131] The Tabernacle—and later the temple—would be located there. God would eventually choose Jerusalem as that place.

Questions to ponder or discuss: When Jesus died, the veil between the Holy of Holies and the Holy Place in the temple was torn in two,[132] symbolizing that we had been reconciled to God and that our separation from him had finally ended. Why do you think we nevertheless sometimes feel separated, or cut off, from God? What should we do at those times?

---

130. See Exodus 25:26-28, 27:4-7, 37:13-15, 37:27-28, 38:5-7.

131. Deuteronomy 12:5 and 12:11

132. See Matthew 27:51, Mark 15:38, and Luke 23:45.

Chapter 28
Tithes and Offerings

(Leviticus chapters 1 – 10, 12, 14 – 16, 19, 22 – 23, 27 – 28; Numbers chapters 6 – 9, 15, 18, 28 – 29; Deuteronomy chapters 14 and 16)

Tithing—that is, giving ten percent of crops, fruits, and newborn animals to God—was mandated in Leviticus 27:30-33, Numbers 18:21-32, and Deuteronomy 14:22-29.

In addition to tithes, the books of Leviticus, Numbers, and Deuteronomy discuss many types of offerings:

burnt offerings
peace offerings
sin offerings
guilt offerings
grain offerings
drink offerings
wave offerings
thanksgiving offerings
freewill offerings
first fruits offerings

Tithes and offerings were intended for the support of the Levites and the priests, who served God in the Tabernacle (and later, the temple). Tithes belonged to the Levites,[133] who were in turn expected to donate ten percent of those tithes—"a tithe of the tithe"[134]—to the priests.[135] In addition, the priests received a portion of each of the offerings listed above—except burnt offerings, which were completely consumed.

---

133. Numbers 18:21-24

134. Numbers 18:26

135. Numbers 18:25-28

Many of these offerings occurred at designated times. What the Pentateuch calls "continual burnt offerings" were made twice each day—once in the morning and again at twilight.[136] In addition to the continual burnt offerings, offerings were required once a week on the Sabbath,[137] at the beginning of each new moon,[138] at the Feast of Trumpets,[139] on the Day of Atonement,[140] and at the three annual festivals: Passover and the Feast of Unleavened Bread,[141] the Feast of Weeks (also known as the Feast of the Harvest),[142] and the Feast of Booths.[143]

Each individual was required to tithe. Most of the offerings were made by the Israelite community as a whole, although individuals might do so to show gratitude to God or to seek his mercy and forgiveness.

These tithes and offerings served at least three purposes: (1) they supported the priests and the Levites who devoted themselves to God's work[144]; (2) they taught the Israelites to put God first in their lives by giving him their very best, since most of these offerings (though *not* the

---

136. Numbers 28:1-8

137. Numbers 28:9-10

138. Numbers 28:11-15 and 29:6

139. Numbers 29:1-6

140. Numbers 29:7-11

141. Numbers 28:16-25

142. Numbers 28:26-31

143. Numbers 29:12-39

144. See Malachi 3:10: " 'Bring the whole tithe into the storehouse, so that there may be food in My house, and test Me now in this,' says the LORD of hosts, 'if I will not open for you the windows of heaven and pour out for you a blessing until it overflows.' "

tithe[145]) had to be free from any defect, disease, or deformity; and (3) they provided atonement and forgiveness for sin, which requires the shedding of blood.[146]

Questions to ponder or discuss: In Malachi 3:8,[147] God accuses the Israelites of "robbing" him by failing to pay their tithes and offerings. What do you think is God's attitude about tithing in the New Testament?

How, if at all, do any the following verses impact your answer: Mark 12:41-44,[148] 2 Corinthians 9:7[149], and Philippians 4:14 and 14:18[150]?

---

145. See Leviticus 27:32-33.

146. See Leviticus 17:11 and Hebrews 9:22.

147. Malachi 3:8: "Will a man rob God? Yet you are robbing Me! But you say, 'How have we robbed You?' In tithes and offerings."

148. Mark 12:41-44: "And He [Jesus] sat down opposite the treasury, and *began* observing how the people were putting money into the treasury; and many rich people were putting in large sums. A poor widow came and put in two small copper coins, which amount to a cent. Calling His disciples to Him, He said to them, 'Truly I say to you, this poor widow put in more than all the contributors to the treasury; for they all put in out of their surplus, but she, out of her poverty, put in all she owned, all she had to live on.' "

149. 2 Corinthians 9:7: "Each one *must* do just as he has purposed in his heart, not grudgingly or under compulsion, for God loves a cheerful giver."

150. Philippians 4:16 and 14:18: "for even in Thessalonica you sent *a gift* more than once for my needs. . . . I am amply supplied, having received from Epaphroditus what you have sent, a fragrant aroma, an acceptable sacrifice, well-pleasing to God."

Chapter 29
Old Testament Criminal Laws
(Exodus chapters 20 – 23; Leviticus chapters 18 – 20 and 24;
Numbers chapters 5, 15, and 35; Deuteronomy chapters 13,
17 – 20, 22, 25, and 27)[151]

Many of the criminal laws in the Pentateuch have direct parallels to our own. For example, the Pentateuch prescribes punishments for murder,[152] kidnapping,[153] assault with serious injury,[154] rape,[155] and theft.[156]

And as we have seen before (chapter nine), the Old Testament absolutely forbid human sacrifice.

Unlike our justice system, the Pentateuch does not mention confinement. This is not surprising, since the Israelites at that time were a nomadic people. The division of Canaan, where they would eventually settle down, was still more than forty years in the future. Jails and prisons would have been impractical. So the prescribed punishments instead included death,[157] physical injury,[158] a financial penal-

---

151. The criminal laws are scattered throughout the books of Exodus, Leviticus, Numbers, and Deuteronomy. These are merely, in my opinion, the most important chapters, and most of these chapters are not devoted exclusively to criminal laws.

152. Numbers 35:30-31

153. Exodus 21:16

154. Leviticus 24:19-20

155. Deuteronomy 22:25-27

156. Exodus 22:1

157. For example, see Exodus 21:12, 14, Leviticus 24:17, 21, Numbers 35:9-34, and Deuteronomy 19:11-13, which impose the death penalty for murder.

158. For example, see Leviticus 24:19-20.

ty,[159] and/or restitution[160] for various types of offenses.

The Pentateuch prescribed punishments for a few offenses that we no longer regard as crimes, such as sorcery, idolatry, and false prophecy. This too is not surprising, since God was trying to teach the Israelites to rely on him rather than on false gods or phony magic. And to teach them proper respect for God, blasphemy was forbidden.

As harsh as Israelite criminal law could be, it was also quite progressive and merciful. For example, it disallowed punishment—and especially the punishment of death—based upon the word of a single witness.[161] A death sentence could be carried out only upon the guilty person, not upon his family members.[162] The law provided a way for a person guilty of unintentionally causing the death of another to escape punishment by fleeing to one of six cities of refuge.[163] And the law sought to ensure justice by prohibiting bribery, false testimony, and the perversion of justice.[164]

Questions to ponder or discuss: Leviticus 20:10[165] mandates the death penalty for a man or woman who commits adultery. How could adultery adversely impact a patriarchal society like the Israelites in which land was allocated and passed to heirs based on a father's family heri-

---

159. For example, see Exodus 21:32 and 22:7.

160. For example, see Exodus 21:33-34 and 22:6.

161. Numbers 35:30, Deuteronomy 17:6, and Deuteronomy 19:15

162. Deuteronomy 24:16

163. Exodus 21:13; Numbers 35:9-15, 22-28; Deuteronomy 19:1-10

164. Exodus 23:1-3, 6-8; Deuteronomy 16:18-20, 19:16-21

165. Leviticus 20:10 says: "If there is a man who commits adultery with another man's wife, one who commits adultery with his friend's wife, the adulterer and the adulteress shall surely be put to death."

tage? What should a Christian's attitude be toward adultery today? How does John 8:1-11[166] affect your answer?

Do you think the death penalty should still be imposed for any type of crime today? Why or why not?

---

166. This is the story of the woman caught in adultery, whom Jesus saved by telling the scribes and Pharisees, "He who is without sin among you, let him be the first to throw a stone at her." While I consider this story to be consistent with the character and teachings of Jesus, it is not contained in the oldest manuscripts of John's gospel, and therefore may not have been part of his original gospel.

Chapter 30
Roots of the Two Greatest Commandments
(Leviticus 19:18; Deuteronomy 6:5)

When Jesus was asked to name the greatest commandment in the Jewish Law, he quoted Deuteronomy 6:5: "You shall love the LORD your God with all your heart and with all your soul and with all your might." Then he quoted Leviticus 19:18 as the second greatest commandment: "you shall love your neighbor as yourself."[167]

The Law has many similar provisions. For example, an Israelite who saw his enemy's animal wandering away was required to return the animal, and if the animal was in distress he must come to its aid.[168]

The Pentateuch mandated that the Israelites show kindness and justice to widows, orphans, strangers, and the poor.[169] Similarly, they were not to mistreat the blind or the deaf,[170] and were to honor the elderly.[171]

The poor and needy were not to be taken advantage of or mistreated, but were instead to be treated with generosity.[172] And if an Israelite became so poor that he sold himself into slavery to another Israelite, the slave was to be treated like a hired man rather than a slave.[173] By the way,

---

167. See Matthew 22:34-40.

168. Exodus 23:4-5

169. Exodus 22:21-22, 23:9; Leviticus 19:9-10, 19:33-34, 23:22; Deuteronomy 24:17-22

170. Leviticus 19:14

171. Leviticus 19:32

172. Leviticus 25:35-38; Deuteronomy 15:7-11

173. Leviticus 25:39-40

all Israelite slaves went free during the Jubilee year, which occurred every fifty years.[174]

Even in business the Israelites were to be fair and honest—false weights and measures were forbidden.[175]

Questions to ponder or discuss: In light of the above, how would you answer those who assert that the Old Testament is harsh and antiquated? How often do we as a society live up to the ideals discussed above?

---

174. Leviticus 25:10-11 and 25:39-41

175. Leviticus 19:35-36; Deuteronomy 25:13-16

Chapter 31
The Clean and the Unclean

(Leviticus chapters 11 –15 and 17; Numbers chapters 5, 19, and 31; Deuteronomy chapters 14 and 23 – 24)

Leviticus 11 and Deuteronomy 14 list the "clean" animals that the Israelites were permitted to eat, as well as "unclean" animals that were forbidden. The clean included animals with split hooves that chew the cud (for example, ox, sheep, goat, and deer); river and sea creatures with fins and scales (that is, most fish); locusts, crickets, grasshoppers, and some birds.

The unclean included, among others: pigs, camels, and rabbits; animals with paws, such as dogs and cats; snakes and other reptiles; predatory and carrion birds; and most insects. In addition, any animal which died a natural death—for example, through disease or old age—was considered unclean.

Most—and perhaps all—of these rules appear to have been based on good nutrition and hygiene, because the unclean meats often carried a risk of toxins, parasites, and/or infection from bacteria or viruses, risks that were usually absent from the clean meats.

A person who touched an unclean animal or its carcass was considered unclean until evening, and objects which came in contact with an unclean animal had to be washed or, in some cases, destroyed. Touching a dead human body rendered a person unclean for a week. These rules, which may seem odd or even arbitrary to us, were necessary because people at that time lacked our modern understanding of how disease-causing germs are spread to humans.

Additional rules regarding "uncleanness" are found in various chapters of Numbers, Leviticus, and Deuteronomy.[176] Most of these rules provided for temporary ceremonial uncleanness, such as for a menstruating woman or a man who had a seminal emission. One exception is Leviticus chapters 13-14, which set forth rules regarding leprosy, a dreaded disease for which people had no cure until relatively modern times.[177] To keep the disease from spreading,[178] the leper was required to live outside the camp.[179]

Questions to ponder or discuss: Several New Testament verses seem to say that these rules regarding unclean foods do not apply to Christians—see, for example, Matthew 15:11, Acts 10:13-15, and Romans 14:14.[180] If God laid down these rules in the interest of our good health, should we follow them anyway? Why or why not?

---

176. See chapters 12 through 15 and 17 of Leviticus; chapters 5, 19, and 31 of Numbers; and chapters 14, 23, and 24 of Deuteronomy.

177. The Bible's references to "leprosy" probably included a variety of other skin diseases, too.

178. According to the U.S. government web site for the Centers for Disease Control and Prevention (https://www.cdc.gov/leprosy), leprosy is spread by close, prolonged contact with an untreated, infected person.

179. Leviticus 13:46

180. Matthew 15:11: "*It is* not what enters into the mouth *that* defiles the man, but what proceeds out of the mouth, this defiles the man."

Acts 10:13-15: "A voice came to him, 'Get up, Peter, kill and eat!' But Peter said, 'By no means, Lord, for I have never eaten anything unholy and unclean.' Again a voice *came* to him a second time, 'What God has cleansed, no *longer* consider unholy.' "

Romans 14:14: "I know and am convinced in the Lord Jesus that nothing is unclean in itself; but to him who thinks anything to be unclean, to him it is unclean."

Chapter 32
The Census and the Camp
(Numbers chapters 1 – 3)

Before leaving Mount Sinai, the Lord directed Moses to take a census of the male Israelites who were at least twenty years old and able to go to war. Thus, those who were too young, too old, or too disabled to fight were not counted. The Levites were also omitted from this census. They would be numbered separately.

Judah was the most numerous tribe, with 74,600 men of fighting age, while the smallest tribe was Manasseh with only 32,200 potential warriors.

The Lord placed the Tabernacle at the center of the Israelite camp, surrounded by the priests and 22,000 Levites. They were in turn surrounded by the other twelve tribes—three tribes on each of the four cardinal points.

Judah camped east of the Tabernacle—along with the tribes of Issachar and Zebulun—where they could protect the priests and the Tabernacle entrance. Those three tribes led the Israelites whenever they broke camp to move. They were followed by the tribes of Gad, Simeon, and Reuben, who camped on the south side of the Tabernacle.

Next came the Levites, who transported the Tabernacle and its contents, including the Ark. As in the camp arrangement, the Ark, the Tabernacle, and the Levites were well protected by being placed in the center of the Israelites' marching formation.

Behind the Levites came the tribes of Ephraim, Manasseh, and Benjamin, who camped to the west of the Tabernacle. Dan, Asher, and Naphtali camped north of the

Tabernacle, broke camp last of all, and protected the Israelites' rear.

Question to ponder or discuss: God directed the priests and the Levites to camp between the Tabernacle and the rest of the Israelites. Part of the reason for this arrangement was surely to keep the Israelites away from the Tabernacle, since Numbers 1:51[181] prohibited them from approaching it. Thus, by placing the Levites between the Tabernacle and the rest of the Israelites, God tried to remove or limit the temptation to disobey this rule. How do you think God tries to help us avoid temptations today?

---

181. Numbers 1:51: "So when the tabernacle is to set out, the Levite shall take it down; and when the tabernacle encamps, the Levites shall set it up. But the layman who comes near shall be put to death."

Chapter 33
Spying on Canaan
(Numbers 10:11 – 14:45)

When the Israelites left Mount Sinai early in the second year after the Exodus from Egypt, they again demonstrated the weakness of their faith in the Lord.

First, at Taberah, they complained of "adversity," and the Lord sent fire to burn part of their camp.[182]

Next they came to Kibroth-hattaavah and complained about the lack of variety in their diet: "There is nothing at all to look at except this manna."[183] Never mind that "this manna" had kept them alive for more than a year. The Lord sent thirty days of quail—along with a plague as punishment for their constant griping and ingratitude.

The Israelites moved on to Kadesh-barnea,[184] from which Moses sent twelve men—one from each of the tribes other than Levi—to secretly explore the land of Canaan to the north. He directed these twelve spies to report back on the nature of the land, the cities, and the people. Forty days later, the spies brought a mixed report: the land was indeed beautiful and fertile, but the cities were walled and well defended, and the people tall and powerful.

Of the twelve men, only two—Joshua and Caleb—expressed confidence in God's ability to bring them victory.[185] The Israelite people sided with the ten who forecast

---

182. Numbers 11:1-3. Numbers does not say that anyone perished in this fire, but only that the fire consumed the outskirts of the camp.

183. Numbers 11:4-6

184. Kadesh-barnea is also known as simply Kadesh. Compare Numbers 13:25-26 and Numbers 32:8.

185. Numbers 13:30 and 14:6-9

gloom and doom, and thus failed another test of faith. They even threatened to stone Joshua and Caleb for their optimism.

At this point the Lord gave up on the generation of Israelites who had followed Moses out of Egypt. God must have decided that they would never have the kind of faith that he required. So he decided to delay the entry into Canaan for forty years, until that generation—everyone age twenty and above—had died out.

Upon hearing the Lord's decision, the people failed yet again. Instead of accepting his judgment, they made a belated attempt to invade Canaan without the Lord's blessing or approval. They were soundly defeated.

Questions to ponder or discuss: After hearing the Lord's rebuke for their lack of faith in the matter of the spies, the Israelites apparently repented—see Numbers 14:39-40.[186] But the Lord still refused to let them enter Canaan. Why do you think he reacted that way? How does Numbers 14:22 (see chapter thirty-four) affect your answer?

If a pardon is defined as "release from punishment," how is forgiveness different from a pardon? Explain.

---

186. Numbers 14:39-40: "When Moses spoke these words to all the sons of Israel, the people mourned greatly. In the morning, however, they rose up early and went up to the ridge of the hill country, saying, 'Here we are; we have indeed sinned, but we will go up to the place which the LORD has promised.' "

Chapter 34
Putting God to the Test
(Numbers 14:22)

In Numbers 14:22, the Lord says that the Israelites "have put Me to the test these ten times" — and he wasn't happy about it. What does putting God to the test mean?

Briefly, it is the opposite of faith. The one who tests God does not trust him.[187]

As God's people, we need to have faith in him.[188] Hebrews 11:1 says that "faith is the assurance of things hoped for, the conviction of things not seen." If seeing is believing, faith is believing without necessarily seeing.

The Israelites tested God ten times because they did not trust him. They lost faith in him whenever they faced difficulties. Numbers does not tell us what those "ten times" were, but I believe they were as follows:

1.   Exodus 5:20-21 – When Moses first confronted Pharaoh and demanded that he let the Israelites go into the wilderness to offer sacrifices to God, Egypt's ruler instead made the Israelites' labor more burdensome.[189] The Israelites' response was to blame Moses for their misfortune. In doing so, they were indirectly blaming God, who had sent Moses.

---

187. In Matthew 4:7, Jesus quotes Deuteronomy 6:16 ("You shall not put the LORD your God to the test") to counter Satan's challenge to throw himself off the top of the temple in Jerusalem. The full quote in Deuteronomy 6:16 includes the phrase, "as you tested *Him* at Massah." Massah refers to Exodus 17:1-7, when the Israelites complained that they had no water to drink.

188. For example, see Habakkuk 2:4, Luke 7:50, Romans 3:28, Romans 5:1, and 2 Corinthians 5:7. Many other examples could be cited.

189. Exodus 5:1-19

2.   Exodus 6:9 – Moses relayed a message from God to the people, assuring them that he would deliver them from their bondage and burdens at the hands of the Egyptians, and would bring them into the land promised to their ancestors.[190] But the people refused to believe Moses when he delivered God's message.

3.   Exodus 14:10-12 – When Pharaoh pursued the Israelites with his army and trapped them against the Sea of Reeds, the people complained to Moses: "Is it because there were no graves in Egypt that you have taken us away to die in the wilderness?"[191] This was of course after they had witnessed God afflict the Egyptians with ten miraculous plagues.

4.   Exodus 15:22-24 – After traveling in the Sinai Peninsula for three days without water, the people "grumbled" at Moses, saying, "What shall we drink?"[192]

5.   Exodus 16:1-3 – About forty-five days into their journey the people again lost faith, accusing Moses of bringing them "out into this wilderness to kill this whole assembly with hunger."[193]

6   Exodus 17:1-2 – At Rephidim the people complained about a lack of water to drink.

7.   Exodus 32:1-4 – With Moses up on Mount Sinai, the people persuaded Aaron to make an idol—a "molten calf"—for them to worship in place of God.

8.   Numbers 11:1-2 – Numbers is vague about exactly what the people did next to anger the Lord, except to say that they "became like those who complain of adversity."

---

190. Exodus 6:1-8

191. Exodus 14:11

192. Exodus 15:24

193. Exodus 16:3

9.   Numbers 11:4-6 – Shortly thereafter, the people complained about the lack of meat to eat, adding: "There is nothing at all to look at except this manna."[194]

10.   Numbers 14:1-4 – Finally, when the spies returned from Canaan with warnings about the strength of the land's cities and people, the Israelites despaired and actually discussed returning to Egypt.

In each instance, the people focused on their circumstances instead of placing their faith in God and his ability to deliver them.

Questions to ponder or discuss: As Christians, we believe that God is able to change our circumstances. Yet experience teaches that he does not always do so. What reason(s) could he have for allowing us to remain in difficult, trying, or even dangerous circumstances? How do verses like Matthew 26:39,[195] 2 Corinthians 11:23-30,[196] and 2 Corinthians 12:7-9[197] impact your answer?

---

194. Numbers 11:6

195. Matthew 26:39: "And He [Jesus] went a little beyond *them*, and fell on His face and prayed, saying, 'My Father, if it is possible, let this cup pass from Me; yet not as I will, but as You will.' "

196. In 2 Corinthians 11:23-30, the apostle Paul talks of the many things he suffered for the cause of Christ, including imprisonments, beatings, and many dangers.

197. In 2 Corinthians 12:7-9, Paul talks about the "thorn in the flesh" that he thrice asked God to remove, but without success.

Chapter 35
Korah's Rebellion
(Numbers chapter 16)

In Numbers 16, a Levite named Korah led a rebellion against Moses' leadership, and was joined by Dathan, Abiram, and 250 leaders of the Israelites. As a Levite, Korah served the priests in the Tabernacle, and as a member of the Kohathites, he was one of those responsible for transporting the Ark and the other Tabernacle furniture from place to place.[198] Numbers 16:10 implies that Korah wanted to be a priest. Korah's pride and jealousy led him to accuse Moses of exalting himself "above the assembly of the LORD," arguing that Moses was nothing special because "all the congregation are holy."[199]

Korah's accusation was foolish. Numbers 12:3 tells us that Moses "was very humble, more than any man who was on the face of the earth." Numbers 11:26-29 provides an example of Moses' humility, for he felt no jealousy when the Lord favored other men with gifts of prophecy, but was instead happy for them.

To appreciate what happened next, we need to understand that Korah's rebellion was not only against Moses and Aaron, but against God. By challenging God's chosen leaders, as well as his plan for the Levites, Korah was defying God. The same was true for those who took Korah's side. Some of them blamed Moses for the fact that they were stuck in the wilderness, even though God, not Moses, had decreed that they should wander in the wilderness for forty years.

---

198. Numbers 3:31

199. Numbers 16:3

Chapter 35 – Korah's Rebellion

Before Korah and his followers could lead the Israelites astray, God destroyed them. The earth opened up and swallowed Korah, Dathan, and Abiram, along with the families and possessions of Dathan and Abiram.[200] Then fire consumed the 250 Israelite leaders who had joined the rebellion.

Incredibly, the people blamed Moses and Aaron for these deaths. So before another rebellion could break out, the Lord sent a plague which was stopped only when Aaron made atonement for the people—after 14,700 more had died.

Questions to ponder or discuss: As with Adam and Eve, disobedience toward God led to death—and in this case, the deaths were almost immediate. Is this a just result? Why or why not?

Korah's rebellion amounted to treason—which is punishable by death in many countries (including the United States until 1990). Does this alter your answer and/or opinion?

---

200. Numbers 16:25-33. Numbers 16:27 mentions only the families of Dathan and Abiram being swallowed up, and Numbers 26:11 explicitly tells us that Korah's sons did not die. (See also the heading for Psalm 88: "A Psalm of the sons of Korah.") Numbers does not explain why Korah's family members were spared.

Chapter 36
Aaron's Staff
(Numbers 17:1 – 17:11)

Even after Korah and his followers had been wiped
out, his rebellion still represented a threat to Moses' leadership because the peoples' underlying grievances against
Moses and Aaron remained—and indeed, had multiplied.

Many were angry about Moses' prophecy that they
would die in the wilderness without reaching the Promised
Land.[201] Some may have blamed Moses for their defeat
against the Amalekites and Canaanites, since Moses had
refused to go with them.[202] They certainly blamed Moses for
the deaths of Korah and his rebel followers,[203] and probably
for the deaths of almost 15,000 more from the plague.[204]
Moses' leadership appeared to have led only to defeat,
death, and despair.

Yet God's next miracle centered around the leadership of Aaron, not Moses. This implies that the grievance
which most concerned the Lord was that of Korah, who
challenged Aaron's preferential status as priest.[205] Recall
that Korah argued that "all the congregation are holy."[206]
The Lord was about to show them that not all are chosen.

At the Lord's direction, Moses instructed Aaron and
eleven other tribal leaders to select a staff and write their
names on them. Then all twelve staffs were placed inside

---

201. Numbers 16:12-14

202. Numbers 14:41-45

203. Numbers 16:41

204. Numbers 16:46-49

205. Numbers 16:8-10

206. Numbers 16:3

the Tent of Meeting, in front of the Ark. Moses predicted that the staff of the Lord's choice would sprout. The next day, Aaron's staff "had sprouted and put forth buds and produced blossoms, and it bore ripe almonds."[207]

After Moses showed it to the people as a sign of the Lord's choice of Aaron as priest, Moses returned it to its place next to the Ark.

Hebrews 9:4 tells us that Aaron's staff was one of three items which were kept in the Ark, the other two being a golden jar containing manna and the tablets on which the Ten Commandments were inscribed.

Questions to ponder or discuss: I am certain I am not being controversial when I say that God loves all of us. Yet in his wisdom he often chooses a single individual to carry out his purposes—for example, Moses, King David, each of the prophets, and Paul. Why do you think God generally works through individuals rather than groups or committees? What do you think he looks for in making such choices?

---

207. Numbers 17:8

Chapter 37
Moses' Critical Mistakes
(Numbers 20:2 –20:13)

The Israelites arrived at (or returned to) Kadesh, where they found no water. Once again they despaired, certain that they would die of thirst in this "wretched place."[208]

The Lord did not get angry this time, for he had a plan that seemed certain to impress the people. He instructed Moses to assemble them and speak to the rock, which would then pour forth water for them to drink.

Sure enough, water did gush from the rock. But Moses angered the Lord because he made two mistakes. First, rather than praising God for the miracle that was about to occur, Moses gave the credit to himself and Aaron: "Listen now, you rebels; shall we bring forth water for you out of this rock?"[209] Second, instead of merely speaking to the rock, as the Lord had instructed, Moses struck the rock with his staff—twice.

Thus, an incredible miracle was cheapened in the people's sight. By striking the rock, Moses allowed the possibility of a naturalistic explanation. And by failing to give God the credit, he exalted himself at God's expense.

For these transgressions, the Lord decreed that Moses would not enter the Promised Land. He would eventually *see* the Promised Land from Mount Pisgah, but he would die before the Israelites entered it.[210]

Questions to ponder or discuss: I believe God still does miracles today. Indeed, my son would not be alive to-

---

208. Numbers 20:5

209. Numbers 20:10

210. Deuteronomy 34:1-5

day without a miracle from God. However, sometimes we miss his miracles because we attribute them to coincidence or good luck. An aphorism wrongly attributed to Albert Einstein says that a coincidence is when God performs a miracle and chooses to remain anonymous.

What miracle(s) has God accomplished for you, or perhaps for someone you know? Have you ever been tempted to cheapen a miracle by describing it to others as a mere coincidence or a natural occurrence? If yes, explain.

Chapter 38
The Journey Around Edom
(Numbers 20:14 –21:9)

Kadesh-barnea was located in the southern portion of what is now Israel, in the desert region known as the Negev, southwest of the Dead Sea. The Jordan River flows south into the Dead Sea, which is below sea level. Because the water in the Dead Sea has nowhere to go, it simply evaporates, leaving behind salt and other minerals that would otherwise flow into the ocean. The Dead Sea is almost ten times as salty as the ocean—so salty that only bacteria and fungi can survive in it.

The land of Edom was south of the Dead Sea. The Edomites were descendants of Esau, who also went by the name, Edom.[211] God had warned the Israelites against provoking the Edomites or attempting to take any of their land.[212] So Moses sent messengers to the king of Edom, requesting permission to simply pass through his land, and promising to take nothing that belonged to the Edomites.

Moses probably hoped to take a short cut to the King's Highway, which was an ancient trade route. A portion of the King's Highway ran north-south through what is now western Jordan, from Aqaba, at the northern tip of the Gulf of Aqaba, to Damascus, Syria and beyond to the Euphrates River. To invade Canaan from the east—as the Israelites would soon do—this was the natural route to take, because the road ran close to the eastern shore of the Jordan River.

---

211. See Genesis 25:30.

212. Deuteronomy 2:4-5

Chapter 38 – The Journey Around Edom

Although the Edomites sold food and water to the Israelites,[213] the king of Edom refused to allow them to pass through his territory, and sent his army to enforce his will. So the Israelites instead detoured south to the Gulf of Aqaba.

Along the way, Aaron died at Mount Hor—which Numbers 20:23 says is on the border of Edom—and was succeeded as high priest by his son, Eleazar.

Because of the long detour around Edom, the Israelites again got mad at Moses—and God. They complained about the lack of water and the lack of food other than manna. So the Lord sent "fiery serpents"—i.e., poisonous snakes—to punish them. But unlike so many times before, this time the people repented. Maybe they had learned a thing or two after forty years in the wilderness.

The Lord told Moses to make a bronze serpent on a pole. Anyone who looked at it did not die if they were bitten by one of the snakes.[214]

Upon reaching the Gulf of Aqaba, the Israelites presumably traveled north along the King's Highway, just east of Edom, until they reached Moab.

Questions to ponder or discuss: Why do you think God led the Israelites east of the Dead Sea instead of having them invade Canaan from the south, as they had unsuccessfully tried to do before (see chapter thirty-three)? Has God ever led you in a different direction after you felt that you had failed him? Explain.

---

213. Deuteronomy 2:4-6 and 2:28-29

214. Numbers 21:8-9. Numbers does not tell us how many people died—only that "many" did. (Numbers 21:6)

Chapter 39
Victory Over the Amorites
(Numbers 21:10 –21:35; Deuteronomy chapters 2 – 3)

Following the King's Highway north from Aqaba, the Israelites passed through the territory of the Moabites, east of the Dead Sea, and close to the territory of the Ammonites, who resided northeast of Moab.[215] These were the descendants of Moab and Ammon, the sons of Lot (Abraham's nephew). The Lord warned Moses not to provoke or harass the Moabites or the Ammonites,[216] so the Israelites passed through Moab peacefully, which brought them to the Arnon River and the land of the Amorites.

The Amorites lived north of Moab. The Arnon River, which flows west into the Dead Sea, was the border between the Amorites and the Moabites. The Amorites were descendants of Canaan, who was a son of Ham and a grandson of Noah.[217]

As he had done with Edom, Moses asked Sihon, an Amorite king, for permission to pass through his territory peacefully, for the Israelites were trying to reach the Jordan River and Canaan. But Sihon refused, and brought his army out to fight.[218] The Israelites triumphed in the ensuing battle and took possession of the Amorites' land east of the Jordan River and west of Ammon, from the Arnon River north to the Jabbok River[219] (which flows west into the Jordan River).

---

215. Deuteronomy 2:8 and 2:19

216. Deuteronomy 2:9 and 2:19

217. Genesis 10:15-16; see also Genesis 9:18 and 10:6

218. Numbers 21:21-23

219. Numbers 21:24-26

Chapter 39 – Victory Over the Amorites

Og king of Bashan, another Amorite king, ruled the territory north of the Jabbok River. Seeing what the Israelites had done to Sihon, Og feared that he would be next. So he attacked the Israelites and was decisively defeated.[220]

As a result of these victories over the Amorites, the Isralites took possession of all of the land east of the Jordan River, from the Arnon River as far north as Mount Herman, northeast of the Sea of Galilee.[221] This land would become the property of the tribes of Reuben, Gad, and Manasseh.[222] Manasseh would also receive land west of the Jordan River, once Canaan had been conquered.

The Israelites were now in position to cross the Jordan River and invade Canaan.

Questions to ponder or discuss: Numbers 21:34-35 says that the Israelites killed all of the Amorites who were living in the conquered territory, and implies that they did so at the Lord's direction. This seems harsh to us now, but we may well ask what alternative they had. If the Israelites had let the Amorites live, how might their situation have been similar to that of modern-day Israel, where the Jewish people live in constant tension with the Palestinians, the most militant of whom want to destroy or expel the Jewish people and get the land back? Do you see a better solution? Explain.

---

220. Numbers 21:33-35

221. Deuteronomy 3:8

222. Deuteronomy 3:12-17

Chapter 40
Balaam
(Numbers chapters 22 – 24)

The story of Balaam is one of the more amusing tales in the Bible. It begins with Balak, the king of Moab. Even though the Israelites had passed through his kingdom peacefully, Balak was dismayed when he saw the Israelites destroy the powerful Amorite kings.

Perhaps realizing that his army was not strong enough to defeat the Israelites, Balak resorted to sorcery. He sent for Balaam, whom Joshua 13:22 identifies as a soothsayer (also translated as a diviner or a magician), and asked him to curse the Israelites. Balaam lived in Pethor, on the Euphrates River in Mesopotamia, far to the north of Moab.[223]

Balak offered Balaam a hefty fee. However, Balaam wisely consulted God, who told him not to go. When Balak increased his offer, Balaam asked God again. This time God told him to go, but on the condition that Balaam speak only what God instructed him to say.

Despite granting Balaam permission to go, the Lord was nevertheless angry with him for going. At least two explanations for this anger seem possible. The more likely reason is that God was offended that Balaam had asked a second time, apparently motivated by pure greed.[224] But another possibility is that God became angry during the long journey because of something Balaam said or did.

In any event, the Lord sent an angel to slay Balaam. Three times the angel, invisible to Balaam, stood in his path

---

223. Numbers 22:5 and Deuteronomy 23:4

224. 2 Peter 2:15 says Balaam "loved the wages of unrighteousness."

ready to strike him down. Each time he was saved by his donkey, who could see what Balaam could not. First the donkey turned aside. Then she stopped and leaned against a wall. Finally she simply lay down. And on each occasion Balaam struck his perceptive donkey.

At this point the Lord gave the donkey the ability to speak, and she asked her master, "What have I done to you, that you have struck me these three times?"[225] As if a talking animal were an everyday occurrence, Balaam had a brief conversation with her. When God finally allowed Balaam to see how close he had come to being killed by the angel, the soothsayer understood.

Thereafter, each time Balak brought Balaam into position to curse the Israelites, he blessed them instead—just as the Lord had instructed him, but much to the frustration of Balak.

Questions to ponder or discuss: They say everyone has a price. Is there an amount of money that would make you disobey God by deliberately committing a sin? Would it matter if the sin were only a "minor" sin? Explain. Why is the temptation of riches sometimes hard to resist?

---

225. Numbers 22:28

Chapter 41
The Temptation of Idolatry
(Numbers 25:1 – 25:13)

One of the dominant themes of the Old Testament is that the Israelites repeatedly fell into idolatry. And in Numbers 25, it happens again.

The Moabites could not have defeated the Israelites in war, but they were able to mislead them in religion. While the Israelites waited at Shittim to invade Canaan, the Moabites invited them to worship and offer sacrifices to the Moabite god, Baal of Peor. Many accepted the invitation.

Of course this angered the Lord, but we need to understand why. A partial explanation is the fact that the pagans of Canaan—and presumably the Moabites too—engaged in detestable practices such as sorcery, temple prostitution,[226] human sacrifice, and even child sacrifice.[227]

They may have even practiced cannibalism, for in the time of Ezekiel, many years later, the Israelites had adopted that particular custom: "For they have committed adultery, and blood is on their hands. Thus they have committed adultery with their idols and even caused their

---

226. Temple prostitution—sometimes called sacred prostitution, cult prostitution, or religious prostitution—involved sexual intercourse or other sex acts performed in conjunction with religious worship, usually involving a temple priest or priestess. Temple prostitution was forbidden by Deuteronomy 23:17.

227. For example, see Deuteronomy 12:29-31 and 18:9-10, 1 Kings 14:24, and Ezekiel 16:20-21. For more on this topic, and additional citations, see chapter seven in my book, *Beyond Blind Faith: Reasons for the Hope We Have (1 Peter 3:15)*, entitled "Is Yahweh an Ogre?"

sons, whom they bore to Me, to pass through *the fire*[228] to them **as food**."[229]

But I believe the problem goes deeper. The most dangerous aspect of idolatry is that it promises to put us in control. If you placate the gods, then they are obligated to give you what you desire: children, prosperity, victory, etc. The gods are like vending machines—make the required offerings and they will dispense what you desire. Thus, the allure of idolatry is similar to the serpent's false promise to Eve: "you will be like God" (Genesis 3:5).

God doesn't work that way. He calls upon us to trust and obey him. We make sacrifices—such as tithes and offerings—from obedience and gratitude, not greed. There is no automatic *quid pro quo*. We believe he is faithful and will fulfill his promises to us, but in his own time and in his own way, not on demand. He does not work at our convenience or on our schedule.

For many of the Israelites that was unsatisfying. Perhaps they wanted immediate gratification, just as we often do. So they turned to the idols that promised quick and certain returns for their investment.

As a result of their unfaithfulness, the Lord instructed Moses to slay the leaders who had led the Israelites into idolatry. In addition, God sent a plague that killed 24,000. The plague was quieted only when Eleazar's son, Phinehas, slew an Israelite who tried to openly cohabitate

---

228. "Pass through the fire" is a euphemism in the Old Testament for human sacrifice. For example, see Ezekiel 16:21: "You slaughtered My children and offered them up to idols by causing them to pass through *the fire*."

229. Ezekiel 23:37 (emphasis added via boldface)

with a pagan Midianite woman. Not only did the Israelite's actions violate the Lord's prohibition against intermarrying with non-Israelites, but the implication is that this Israelite was defiantly flaunting his lack of remorse and his opposition to Moses' leadership since he did so "in the sight of all the congregation," and while the Israelites were "weeping at the door of the tent of meeting."[230]

The Lord rewarded Phinehas for his faith and obedience by making him and his descendants "a perpetual priesthood."[231]

Questions to ponder or discuss: What is the difference between an idol and a symbol (such as the cross)? Can a symbol become an object of idolatry? Explain.

I believe God *always* answers our prayers, but sometimes his answer is "no" or "not yet." James 4:2-3 says we do not receive what we desire because we do not ask God for it, or because we ask with improper motives. What might be some other reasons why God does not say "Yes" to some of our prayers? (Hint: Paul provides one answer in 2 Corinthians 12:9-10, which is quoted on page thirteen.)

---

230. Numbers 25:6

231. Numbers 25:13

Chapter 42
The Second Census
(Numbers 26:1 –27:11)

As the Israelites prepared to invade Canaan, the Lord ordered another census of all males who were age twenty and above, "whoever is able to go out to war in Israel."[232] This was necessary because all but three of the adult males who had been alive at the time of the first census were now dead—those three being, of course, Moses, Joshua, and Caleb. A second census was also necessary because Canaan was to be divided unevenly, with the larger tribes receiving more land and the less numerous tribes receiving smaller portions of land.[233] So the Israelites needed to determine how many men were in each tribe.

This second census yielded results similar to that of the first census: the Israelite army had more than 600,000 potential soldiers.

As before, the Levites were numbered separately, for they belonged to the Lord. That census revealed 23,000 male Levites above the age of one month.

The census only counted males, so the daughters of Zelophehad brought an inequity to Moses' attention. Their father, as a member of the tribe of Manasseh, would have been entitled to a share of the land, except that he had died in the wilderness. His sons would normally have received

---

232. Numbers 26:2

233. Numbers 26:52-56 and 33:54

his share, except that he had no sons. So his daughters contended that they should receive their father's portion, lest the family be left with nothing. The Lord agreed, but with one stipulation: to ensure that the land would always remain within the tribe of Manasseh, the daughters must marry within their own tribe.[234] This became the rule for the land of any man who died with only daughters to inherit from him.

Keeping the land within the tribe to which it was allocated led to at least two other peculiar rules. First, if a man died before his wife had produced a son to inherit from him, the man's brother was required to marry the widow, and the resulting child would be regarded as the child of the deceased brother.[235]

Second, land could never be permanently sold, but only leased for a term of years. In the Jubilee Year, which was every fiftieth year, all land reverted back to its original owner or his descendants.[236]

Questions to ponder or discuss: Leviticus 25:23 justifies the Jubilee Year rule by explaining that the land belongs to the Lord. How different would our society be if we followed the Jubilee Year rule? What changes would be necessary if we adopted that rule?

---

234. Numbers 36:1-12

235. Deuteronomy 25:5-10

236. Leviticus 25:8-16 and 25:23-24

Chapter 43
The Tribes East of the Jordan River
(Numbers chapter 32)

The Israelite victories over the Amorites had given them an unplanned windfall: a large amount of land east of the Jordan River (in what is now the country of Jordan). This land was perfect for raising livestock, and the tribes of Reuben and Gad had a lot of livestock. So they asked Moses to give them this land instead of a portion in Canaan.

And they asked for another favor: "do not take us across the Jordan."[237] The purpose of this request is unclear. Did they mean they wanted to avoid fighting in Canaan, or merely that they wanted to live east of the Jordan River when the fighting was over? Moses assumed the former, and therefore was indignant. He practically accused the Reubenites and Gadites of cowardice and treachery.

Faced with Moses' accusations the leaders of the two tribes quickly clarified their intent, or perhaps backtracked from their previous position, depending on how their request is interpreted. They explained that they would send their warriors to fight alongside their brothers, leaving behind their families and possessions, and would not return until the war to conquer Canaan was finished. With this assurance Moses approved their plan.

So the tribes of Reuben and Gad, along with the tribe of Manasseh, took possession of the land that had belonged to the Amorites. Manasseh would be given land in Canaan, too, becoming the only tribe with land on both sides of the Jordan River.[238]

---

237. Numbers 32:5

238. See Joshua 17.

These three tribes sent 40,000 warriors to help conquer Canaan.[239] Although Reuben, Gad, and Manasseh combined had almost 137,000 adult males, according to the second census,[240] Joshua was apparently satisfied with their contribution, for nowhere does the Bible hint that they had not lived up to their promise to help their fellow Israelites conquer Canaan.

Questions to ponder or discuss: Since Joshua did not object to the number of warriors sent by the eastern tribes, I think we can safely assume that these were their best fighters. Those who remained east of the Jordan River were probably the soldiers who were older, injured, and/or less capable. Assuming this was the case, the tribes east of the Jordan River exhibited great faith, because sending their best warriors off to war left their families and possessions primarily dependent on God for their security.

Have you faced difficult times when you had to rely primarily on God to take care of yourself and/or your loved ones? (For example, maybe you lost a job, were sent far from home, or were seriously injured.) What happened when you did? What advice would you offer to people who are going through such times?

---

239. Joshua 4:12-13

240. See Numbers 26:7, 26:18, and 26:34.

Chapter 44
Cities of the Levites
(Numbers chapter 35)

The Levites were unlike the other Israelite tribes in several ways. In the Israelite camp, the Levites camped around the Tabernacle. They set it up and transported it, and the members of other tribes were not permitted to come near the Tabernacle, on pain of death.[241] The Levites were entitled to the tithes.

They were also different in that they did not receive land in Canaan. Instead, they received forty-eight cities, along with pasture lands outside the cities for their flocks and herds.[242] These cities were located within the territories of the other tribes.

Six of these forty-eight cities were designated as "cities of refuge." Three of the six were east of the Jordan River:

Bezer, in the territory of Reuben,
Ramoth-gilead, in the territory of Gad, and
Golan, in the territory of Manasseh.[243]

The other three were in Canaan, west of the Jordan:

Kedesh, in Naphtali,
Shechem, in Ephraim, and
Kiriath-arba, also known as Hebron, in Judah.[244]

These six cities of refuge provided a safe haven for anyone who had accidentally or unintentionally killed

---

241. See Numbers 1:51.

242. Numbers 35:1-7 (see also Joshua 21:1-42)

243. Numbers 35:14, Joshua 20:8

244. Numbers 35:14, Joshua 20:7

another person. The victim's family members could not take revenge against the "manslayer" so long as he stayed within a city of refuge. But if he left the city, he could be killed by the victim's family with impunity. The manslayer's exile would end—allowing him to return home—only upon the death of the high priest.[245]

A city of refuge would not protect a murderer who killed someone intentionally or with premeditation. Such a murderer was to be put to death.

Questions to ponder or discuss: Numbers 35:24 and Joshua 20:6 tell us that "the congregation" would judge whether the killer was a manslayer who was entitled to the protection of the city of refuge or a murderer who deserved to die. The Old Testament does not clarify exactly who "the congregation" was, but no single individual appears to have been responsible for the decision. What are the advantages of having a group make this decision rather than one person? What are the disadvantages, if any, to this procedure?

What does this tell you about the wisdom of America's system of trial by jury? When making important decisions in your own life, do you prefer to make them alone or only after consulting with others? Explain.

---

245. Numbers 35:15, 22-28, and Joshua 20:1-6. Using the death of the high priest provided a definite, unambiguous date on which all manslayers could return home, without the need for detailed records or calculations.

Chapter 45
The Death of Moses
(Numbers 27:15 – 17:23; Deuteronomy chapters 31 – 34)

Much of the book of Deuteronomy consists of Moses speaking to the Israelites—recounting some of their journeys, reminding them about many of God's laws, and exhorting them to be faithful and obedient to the Lord. Deuteronomy ends with Moses' death on Mount Nebo, across from Jericho, at the age of 120.[246] Moses had been preceded in death by his sister, Miriam,[247] and his brother, Aaron.

Before he died, Moses commissioned Joshua as his successor, as the Lord had instructed.[248] Moses also wrote down the laws that God had given him and entrusted them to the care of the Levites.[249] Finally, he blessed each tribe of the Israelites.[250]

When he had finished, Moses walked up Mount Nebo,[251] where the Lord showed him all of the land which would one day belong to the Israelites.[252] But because of Moses' disobedience at Kadesh, the Lord had decreed that Joshua, not Moses, would lead the people into the Promised Land.[253] Moses died and was buried in the land of Moab.[254]

---

246. Deuteronomy 34:5, 7

247. Numbers 20:1

248. Numbers 27:15-23; Deuteronomy 31:23

249. Deuteronomy 31:24-26

250. Deuteronomy 33

251. Mount Nebo is also known as Mount Pisgah. See Deuteronomy 34:1.

252. Deuteronomy 34:1-4

253. Deuteronomy 32:48-52

254. Deuteronomy 34:5-6

Questions to ponder or discuss: Just like Moses' mistakes at Kadesh, our poor choices have consequences, often unforeseen and frequently undesired. This does not necessarily mean that God is punishing us like he did with Moses, but merely that bad decisions usually come with a cost. What are some poor choices you have made in the past, and what were the resulting consequences? What did you learn from those experiences? What does this tell you about why God might not want to protect us from the consequences of our poor choices?

Chapter 46
Joshua
(Joshua 1:1 – 1:9)

Jesus' Hebrew name, Yeshua, was a shortened or alternative form of Yehoshu'a (or Jehoshu'a)—in English, Joshua. The name means "Jehovah [the Lord] is salvation."

We first met Joshua the son of Nun in Exodus 17, when Moses directed him to lead a counter-attack against the cowardly Amalekites, who had attacked the Israelite stragglers fleeing from Egypt.

Although Exodus refers to Joshua as Moses' "servant" or "assistant,"[255] depending on the translation, he appears to have been more like a right-hand man. He accompanied Moses at least partway up Mount Sinai when he received the Ten Commandments,[256] and remained at the Tent of Meeting whenever Moses was absent, perhaps as a guard or caretaker.[257]

When Moses sent twelve spies into the land of Canaan, Joshua went as the representative of the tribe of Ephraim.[258] Of the twelve, only Joshua and Caleb expressed confidence in the ability of the Lord to lead the Israelites to victory. As a result the Lord allowed those two to survive and enter Canaan forty years later.[259]

---

255. Exodus 24:13, 33:11

256. Exodus 24:12-14

257. Exodus 33:11

258. Numbers 13:8

259. Numbers 26:63-65

Prior to the Israelites' invasion of Canaan, the Lord selected Joshua as Moses' successor. But Joshua was not quite ready to lead. The Lord first needed to prepare him.

After giving him his marching orders—"arise, cross this Jordan, you and all this people, to the land which I am giving to them"[260]—the Lord tried to instill confidence:

> No man will be able to stand before you all the
> days of your life. Just as I have been with Mos-
> es, I will be with you; I will not fail you or for-
> sake you.[261]

Three times the Lord urged Joshua to "be strong and courageous,"[262] as did Moses before he died.[263] Finally, the Lord reminded Joshua to remain faithful and obedient to God's law.

After receiving these instructions, encouragement, and reminder, Joshua was ready to lead the Israelites to victory.

Questions to ponder or discuss: I once heard a pastor[264] describe faith as *Action* based upon *Belief* supported by *Confidence*—the ABCs of faith. How do you see the ABCs of faith reflected in the Lord's preparation of Joshua to lead the Israelites? How do you see the ABCs of faith reflected in your own life?

---

260. Joshua 1:2

261. Joshua 1:5

262. Joshua 1:6, 1:7, 1:9

263. Deuteronomy 31:7, 31:23

264. Dr. Gene Scott, whom I mentioned in the Preface.

Chapter 47
Preparing for the Battle of Jericho
(Joshua 1:10 –5:12)

Having received his marching orders and assurances of victory from the Lord, Joshua took command and ordered the Israelites to prepare to cross the Jordan River into Canaan. Then he secretly sent two spies to Jericho to observe the city and the surrounding land. A common prostitute—in other words, not a temple prostitute—named Rahab gave them lodging and hid them when Jericho's king sent men to find them. She even lied to the king's men, telling them that the two spies had already departed the city. She later told the spies how to escape undetected.

But what Rahab said may have been even more valuable than what she did, for she told the two Israelite spies that the inhabitants of Jericho were terrified of them. This must have been a big confidence booster for Joshua and the Israelites.

In return for her help, Rahab asked only for the safety of herself and her family when the Israelites attacked. The spies readily agreed, so long as she would gather her family into one house and tie a cord of scarlet thread in her window to ensure that the Israelites would know which house to spare.

When the time came to cross the Jordan River, the Ark of the Covenant led the way, carried by the priests. The involvement of the priests demonstrated to the Israelites that this occasion was something special, because the Kohathites—a branch of the tribe of Levi—normally carried the Ark.[265]

---

265. Numbers 4:15

When the priests' feet touched the river, the water stopped upstream at the city of Adam. (This was not quite the same as what happened at the Sea of Reeds, where the waters simply parted.) This stoppage could have been due to an earthquake upstream. In the past earthquakes have caused the riverbanks to cave in and temporarily dam up the river. But even if that is the explanation, the miracle was in the timing, for the river stopped flowing just when the Israelites needed it to.

The priests stood in the middle of the riverbed with the Ark while the people crossed over. Joshua ordered that the warriors of Reuben, Gad, and Manasseh would cross first, probably because they were not encumbered with families and possessions, and thus would be able to quickly provide any assistance or protection that might be needed.

Joshua 3:15 and 4:18 tell us that the river was at flood stage, so a suddenly resurgent river during the crossing would have been terrifying—and dangerous. In addition, the people must have realized that, once they were across and the swollen river resumed flowing, they would have no retreat if they were defeated. Thus, they displayed great faith by merely agreeing to cross, and again during the actual crossing. This demonstrates how far the Israelites had come since their forefathers' cowardice and hesitation forty years earlier.

When all were safely across, the Lord instructed Joshua to have twelve men—one from each tribe—haul large stones from the dry riverbed. They used these twelve stones to construct a memorial along the shore to remind the Israelites and their children of what the Lord had done for them.[266]

---

266. Joshua 4:1-7

Chapter 47 – Preparing for the Battle of Jericho

At Gilgal, on the western shore of the Jordan, the Israelite males were circumcised—for that had not been done during their forty years in the wilderness. On the fourteenth day of the month they celebrated the Passover. The next day they ate what they found in Canaan—and on that day the manna ceased.

Question to ponder or discuss: Just as the stone memorial reminded the Israelites of the miracle that enabled them to cross the flood-swollen Jordan River, Jesus gave us communion to help us remember him and what he did for us. Why do you think God gives us reminders like those?

Chapter 48
Jericho and Ai
(Joshua chapters 6 – 8)

The story of Jericho is a proud moment in the faith journey of the Israelites. Imagine being told to walk around a city without making a sound—and to do the same thing for six straight days. As if this were not odd enough, on the seventh day you are told to silently walk around the city *seven* times. And then on cue, everyone yells.

Those were the instructions Joshua received from the Lord, which he passed on to the people. And they did it. No questions, no talking back, no grumbling. They simply did it.

When the people shouted on the seventh day, the walls of Jericho fell and the city was easily taken. All of its people and animals were slain, with the sole exception of Rahab and her family.

Joshua had told the Israelites that they were to take no plunder from Jericho. All precious metals like gold, silver, bronze, and iron were to go into the Lord's treasury. This was presumably because under the Law the first fruits belonged to God, and by extension to the priests.[267] Jericho was the first fruits from the invasion of Canaan.

The Israelites dutifully obeyed this injunction against taking loot from Jericho—all except one person, that is. Achan, from the tribe of Judah, took a gold bar, two-

---

267. Exodus 23:19, 34:26; Leviticus 23:10, 23:17; Numbers 18:12-13; Deuteronomy 18:4, 26:1-4

hundred shekels of silver, and "a beautiful mantle[268] from Shinar," which he hid in his tent.

After their victory, the Israelites sent a small force of about 3,000 men to seize the nearby city of Ai. This town had only 12,000 inhabitants, so the Israelites anticipated a swift and easy campaign. They were soundly defeated. Thirty-six Israelites lost their lives. The Lord explained to Joshua that this defeat was the result of Achan's sin. Because of this, Achan, his children, and his animals were stoned to death.

The second battle of Ai went much better for the Israelites. With the Lord's assurance of victory this time, Joshua set a trap. He sent part of his army to wait in ambush behind the city while the rest of the Israelite warriors pretended to flee from battle as before. When Ai emptied the city of soldiers in pursuit of the retreating Israelites, those lying in ambush attacked the city and set it on fire. The soldiers of Ai were doomed. With their retreat cut off, they found themselves caught between the two Israelite armies, and were cut to pieces.

After confiscating cattle and other booty, Joshua hanged Ai's king and burned the city. Then he built an altar to the Lord and read the words of God's law to the people.

Questions to ponder or discuss: Does it seem fair that Achan's children were stoned along with their father? The Bible provides few details, but how would it affect your answer if:

— the children were all adults?
— they were complicit in either stealing or hiding the booty?

---

268. A mantle is a robe or cloak. Shinar refers to Babylonia. See Genesis 10:10, which states that Babel was "in the land of Shinar." Shinar is where the Tower of Babel was located, per Genesis 11:2.

The Old Testament Made Simple (Part 1)

How likely is it that Achan could have done this without his children's knowledge? Would their allegiance to God require that they turn their father in? If you had to choose between God and family, what would you do? Explain.

Chapter 49
The Gibeonites
(Joshua 9:1 – 10:6)

Canaan in the time of Joshua consisted of independent city-states which were nominally beholden to Egypt—in the sense that they paid tribute to the Egyptians, but were otherwise pretty much left to themselves.

When the kings of the city-states in the southern portion of Canaan saw what had happened to Jericho and Ai, they banded together to fight the Israelite invasion—well, all except one.

The city of Gibeon[269] was located west of Jericho and Ai, and north of Jerusalem. Three other cities were associated with Gibeon and probably under Gibeon's control: Chephirah, Beeroth, and Kiriath-jearim. The Gibeonites refused to ally themselves with the southern kings, but instead arranged a ruse in an effort to make peace with the Israelites.

The Gibeonites sent a delegation to Gilgal, the site of the Israelite encampment. These envoys donned worn out shoes and clothing, and carried provisions which appeared to be old.

Then they lied.

They said they had come from far away to make peace with the Israelites, and claimed that their clothing was new and their provisions were fresh when they had begun their journey.

The Israelites fell for it. Without consulting the Lord, Joshua and the Israelites made a peace treaty and an alliance with the Gibeonites. Three days later the Israelites realized they had been tricked, but by then it was too late. They had

---

269. Joshua 11:19

The Old Testament Made Simple (Part 1)

already given their word and "sworn to them by the LORD the God of Israel."[270] So they let the Gibeonites live, but turned them into servants.

However, that was not the end of the story. When the southern kings learned that Gibeon had betrayed them, they decided to attack the Gibeonites, who then called upon their new ally for help. This set the stage for the Israelites' battle at Gibeon against the southern alliance.

Questions to ponder or discuss: James warns us that we should always make our plans with the understanding that they are subject to the Lord's will.[271] When Paul left Ephesus, he promised to return "if God wills."[272] Yet the Israelites failed to seek God's will before making a treaty with the Gibeonites.

Like the Israelites, we often make plans without considering what God's will might be. Why do you believe we do this? What are the advantages and disadvantages of consulting God and/or his word before making important decisions?

---

270. Joshua 9:18-20
271. James 4:13-15
272. Acts 18:21

Chapter 50
The Southern Campaign
(Joshua 10:7 – 10:43)

The kings of five city-states in southern Canaan formed an alliance to oppose the Israelite invasion: Jerusalem, Hebron, Jarmuth, Lachish, and Eglon. The armies of these five kings attacked the Israelites' ally, Gibeon, which sent a plea for help to Joshua.

Rushing to the aid of his ally, Joshua marched his warriors all night and launched a surprise attack against the southern allies at Gibeon. With the Lord's help, the Israelites routed the allied armies, and as they fled the Lord killed many more with large hailstones.

At some point during the battle, Joshua asked the Lord to make the sun stand still so the battle could continue—Joshua 10:13 tell us that the sun stopped for about a day. A possible alternate translation of this verse is that Joshua asked the Lord to make the sun stop beating down so hard, reducing the solar heat so that the Israelites would not get tired and could continue the fight. This would mean the Lord sent thick clouds, or even a storm, to block the sun's rays. A storm would also explain the large hailstones. However, this would not explain Joshua 10:14, which says, "There was no day like that before it or after it," nor does it explain why Joshua 10:13 also says "the moon stopped."

With the southern allies' armies demolished and their best warriors dead, only the mopping up remained. Joshua publicly executed the five kings, who were found hiding in a cave. Then he captured each southern city one by one, killing all of the inhabitants as he did so.

The Old Testament Made Simple (Part 1)

Afterward, Joshua and the Israelite warriors returned to their camp at Gilgal.[273] The women and children had presumably stayed there when Joshua led the army to Gibeon. This interlude allowed the warriors to reunite with their families while they rested and planned the northern campaign.

Questions to ponder or discuss: As they did with the Amorites, the Israelites killed all of the inhabitants of southern Canaan who did not flee. While this seems appalling and shocking from a worldly standpoint, how might verses like 1 Peter 3:18-20[274] and 1 Peter 4:6[275] alter our perspective?

In the case of the flood and Sodom, God destroyed evil himself. Here the Lord uses Joshua and the Israelites to destroy the wicked, idolatrous Canaanites. Why do you think the Lord hates evil so much that he destroys the people who practice it?

---

273. Joshua 4:19, 10:43

274. 1 Peter 3:18-20:

> For Christ also died for sins once for all, *the* just for *the* unjust, so that He might bring us to God, having been put to death in the flesh, but made alive in the spirit; in which also He went and made proclamation to the spirits *now* in prison, who once were disobedient, when the patience of God kept waiting in the days of Noah, during the construction of the ark, in which a few, that is, eight persons, were brought safely through *the* water.

275. 1 Peter 4:6:

> For the gospel has for this purpose been preached even to those who are dead, that though they are judged in the flesh as men, they may live in the spirit according to *the will of* God.

Chapter 51
The Northern Campaign
(Joshua chapter 11)

Like the kings in southern Canaan, those in the north banded together to try to stop the Israelites. These included, among others, the kings of Hazor, Madon, Shimron, and Achshaph. A vast army was assembled, made even more formidable by the presence of horses and chariots—military technology which the Israelites lacked.

Once again God gave Joshua assurance of victory, but this time the Lord added further instructions—after the battle Joshua was to burn the chariots and hamstring the horses, making them useless for war.

The northern alliance armies were camped at the "waters of Merom."[276] Merom was located northwest of the Sea of Galilee, which was then known as the Sea of Chinneroth (or Chinnereth). Joshua launched another surprise attack and destroyed his enemies. Those soldiers who didn't flee were killed. Joshua then easily captured the cities that remained, killing the inhabitants and seizing their possessions. He burned the city of Hazor, which had been the leader of the other cities.

Thus, Joshua completed the conquest of Canaan, except for some isolated pockets of resistance, which are listed in Joshua 17:11-12 and Judges 1:27-34.

After about five years, "the land had rest from war."[277] We know that the Israelites had been fighting for about five years because of Joshua 14:6-10, which says that Caleb was forty years old when Moses sent him and eleven

---

276. Joshua 11:5

277. Joshua 11:23

other Israelites to spy on the land of Canaan, and eighty-five years old at the end of the wars in Canaan—a difference of forty-five years. Since forty of those years were spent in the wilderness, the wars against the Amorites and the Canaanites must have consumed about five years.

Questions to ponder or discuss: Surely the Israelites would have preferred to save the Canaanite horses and chariots for future battles rather than destroy them. Yet such weapons would have been of little use without a professional army trained to use them, which the Israelites did not then possess. What other reason(s) might God have had for requiring the Israelites to destroy the chariots and maim the horses? Have you ever felt called by God to do something you were reluctant to do? How did it work out? Explain.

Chapter 52
Dividing the Promised Land
(Joshua chapters 15 – 19)

With Canaan conquered, Joshua divided the land among the remaining nine and one-half tribes. (The other tribes—Reuben, Gad, and the "half-tribe" of Manasseh[278]—had already settled on land seized from the Amorites, east of the Jordan River.)

If you want to read the details of the division of land, they are spelled out in chapters fifteen through nineteen of Joshua. But briefly, Judah, Benjamin, and Simeon received land in southern Canaan, while the remaining tribes lived further north. Judah's territory included the city of Jerusalem.

As mandated in Numbers 35, the Levites received forty-eight cities within the territories of the other tribes, including the six cities of refuge.[279]

In recognition of Caleb's faithfulness to the Lord, Joshua awarded him the city of Hebron, in the territory of Judah.[280] (Caleb was one of the twelve men sent to spy on the land of Canaan.) Caleb drove out the inhabitants of Hebron, and then turned his attention to the nearby city of Debir, offering the hand of his daughter Achsah to whoever could capture Debir. The man who accomplished this task was

---

278. Manasseh was the only tribe which received land on both sides of the Jordan River. The Bible often uses the term "half-tribe" to refer to the portion of Manasseh living on one side of the river or the other. See for example, Numbers 32:33 and 34:14; Deuteronomy 3:13 and 29:8; and Joshua 1:12, 4:12, 12:6, 13:7-8, 13:29, 14:2-3, 18:7, 21:5-6, 21:25, and 21:27.

279. Joshua 20:1 - 21:42

280. Joshua 14:6-15

Caleb's nephew, Othniel, whom we will meet again in the book of Judges.

Questions to ponder or discuss: In Numbers 26:52-56, the Lord directed that the land was to be divided unevenly, with the more populous tribes receiving more land. How fair do you think that was? What would be the advantages and disadvantages of such an arrangement?

Can you be "fair" to your children without treating each of them the same way? Why or why not?

Chapter 53
An Almost Tragic Misunderstanding
(Joshua chapter 22)

The armies of Canaan were defeated, so Joshua sent the warriors of Reuben and Gad and the half-tribe of Manasseh back across the Jordan River to their families, lands, and possessions.

Before crossing the Jordan and going home, these tribes erected an altar along the banks of the river. Significantly, this altar resembled the one in the Court of the Tabernacle on which the Israelites offered sacrifices to God.

Recall that the Lord had directed all sacrifices to be offered at the location he would choose—*and nowhere else.* The altar constructed by the eastern tribes appeared to violate this mandate. Remembering the Lord's harsh discipline of them on so many other occasions—most recently with Achan—the tribes west of the Jordan River prepared for war, ready to crush this apparent sacrilege. But before marching off to war they prudently sent a delegation led by Phinehas, the son of Eleazar the priest.

The tribes of Reuben, Gad, and Manasseh explained to Phinehas that their altar was not for the purpose of offering sacrifices, but only to serve as a witness that their descendants were followers of the Lord just like those Israelites west of the river. This explanation satisfied everyone. Thus, war was averted and peace prevailed.

Questions to ponder or discuss: When we reach a conclusion hastily, why are we so frequently wrong? How can we avoid jumping to the wrong conclusion?

Misunderstandings between people happen all the time, and perhaps they are inevitable. How can we make them less frequent?

Chapter 54
The Death of Joshua
(Joshua chapters 23 – 24)

Joshua knew his life was nearing its end so he did what he could to ensure that the Israelites would remain faithful to God when he was gone.

Gathering all the people at Shechem, which was centrally located in Palestine,[281] he assured them that the Lord would continue to give them victories over the remaining inhabitants of Palestine until the land was devoid of them. But this assurance was subject to a condition: the Israelites must not associate with, or intermarry with, the Canaanites, for God had forbidden this in Exodus 34:12-16 and Deuteronomy 7:3. Joshua foresaw, as did the Lord, that close association with the Canaanites would inevitably lead to the adoption of their barbaric religious practices. Joshua warned his people against such idolatry, which would bring upon them God's wrath instead of his favor.

Next, Joshua reminded them of all that God had done for them and their ancestors. And he presented them with this famous choice:

---

281. Since at this point in our story Canaan has been conquered and therefore has effectively ceased to exist, I will henceforth use the term "Palestine" or "Israel" to refer to what was once Canaan—and is today Israel—except when I refer to the land as it was prior to the Israelite conquest. After Solomon's death, his empire was divided into a northern kingdom, which became known as Israel, and a southern kingdom known as Judah. (We will cover that in Part Two of *The Old Testament Made Simple*.) Prior to that time, however, the term "Israel" was often used in the Bible to refer to all of Palestine, and was sometimes used to refer to only the northern portion of Palestine. I will continue to refer to the Gentile residents of Palestine as "Canaanites."

If it is disagreeable in your sight to serve the LORD, choose for yourselves today whom you will serve: whether the gods which your fathers served which were beyond the River, or the gods of the Amorites in whose land you are living; but as for me and my house, we will serve the LORD.[282]

In the face of Joshua's repeated warnings that unfaithfulness to God would bring his wrath upon them, the people three times promised to serve the Lord.[283] They memorialized this renewal of their covenant with the Lord by erecting a large stone at Shechem.

Sometime after this, Joshua died at age 110, and was buried within the territory of his tribe, Ephraim.

Joshua 24:31 adds that "Israel served the LORD all the days of Joshua and all the days of the elders who survived Joshua. . . ."[284] But as we will soon see, the Israelites' loyalty to God did not last long after that.

Questions to ponder or discuss: Should Christians only marry within their own religion? What are the dangers of Christians marrying non-believers?

We all face the choice of whom we will serve: God or the world. What does it mean to serve "the world"? Is anything—or anyone—more important to you than your rela-

---

282. Joshua 24:15

283. Joshua 24:18, 24:21, and 24:24

284. See also Judges 2:7

tionship with God? What do you think Matthew 22:36-38[285] and Matthew 10:37[286] say about that?

---

285. In Matthew 22:36-38, Jesus says the greatest commandment in the Jewish law is to "Love the Lord your God with all your heart, and with all your soul, and with all your mind" (from Deuteronomy 6:5).

286. Matthew 10:37 says (Jesus speaking): "He who loves father or mother more than Me is not worthy of Me; and he who loves son or daughter more than Me is not worthy of Me."

Chapter 55
A New Generation Arises
(Judges 1:1 –3:6)

As we have noted before (chapter fifty-one), a few pockets of resistance remained after the Israelites' victories over the southern and northern Canaanite armies. But the Israelites did not drive out or destroy these remaining Canaanites—particularly in the territories of Manasseh, Ephraim, Zebulun, Asher, Naphtali, and Dan.[287]

The Bible does not explain this failure. The most obvious explanation—that the Israelites were unable to do so—seems unlikely. Joshua 17:13 says that "when the sons of Israel became strong, they put the Canaanites to forced labor, but they did not drive them out completely."[288] This implies that the Israelites chose to let the Canaanites stay.

Furthermore, Joshua said that God had fulfilled his promise to bring the people victory over the Canaanites,[289] and assured them of future victories if they remained faithful.[290] Judges 1:1-26 describes some of those victories.

If the Israelites were capable of driving out the Canaanite, why didn't they?

Perhaps they grew tired of fighting. Maybe they felt sorry for the Canaanites, or simply became friends with them. We don't know. But we do know that God had repeatedly warned his people not to associate with the Canaanites, or intermarry with them, lest they become "a snare and a

---

287. Joshua 17:11-13 and Judges 1:27-34

288. Judges 1:28 is similar. And see Joshua 16:10.

289. Joshua 23:9-10 and 23:14

290. Joshua 23:5

trap to you, and a whip on your sides and thorns in your eyes."[291]

That is exactly what happened.

After Joshua and his generation had died off, Judges 2:10 tells us that "there arose another generation after them who did not know the LORD, nor yet the work which He had done for Israel." That generation worshiped the false gods of the Canaanites and adopted their evil practices.

Because of the Israelites' idolatry and wickedness, they lost the Lord's favor. They suffered defeats. Their enemies plundered and oppressed them. Each time the people drifted into idolatry God allowed them to suffer until they recognized their wrongdoing, repented, and sought his help. Then he sent "judges" to deliver them from their enemies.

The Israelites repeated this pattern through many generations in the book of Judges: idolatry, oppression and defeat, repentance, deliverance, and a return to idolatry.

The first judge to provide such deliverance was Othniel, the nephew and son-in-law of Caleb, and the conqueror of Debir.

Questions to ponder or discuss: Why do you think idolatry appealed to young Israelites who had not experienced the victories, defeats, and miracles that Joshua's generation lived through? Why do you think young people so often reject their parents' values and beliefs?

---

291. Joshua 23:13; see also Exodus 23:33 and 34:12, and Deuteronomy 7:16.

Chapter 56
The First Two Judges: Othniel and Ehud
(Judges 2:20 –3:30)

When the generation after Joshua turned away from the Lord, he stopped helping them drive out the Canaanites and the other inhabitants of the land. Instead, he left those peoples in the land to test the Israelites, "to find out if they would obey the commandments of the LORD."[292]

They failed the test.

They intermarried with the local peoples and worshiped their gods. They practiced evil and forgot the Lord. So God allowed them to be conquered and oppressed for eight years by a Mesopotamian king, Cushan-rishathaim, which means "doubly wicked Cushan."

The Israelites asked the Lord for deliverance, and he provided it in the form of Othniel, Caleb's nephew and son-in-law. Othniel defeated Cushan-rishathaim and ushered in forty years of peace.

When those forty years were over and the Israelites again turned to evil, God allowed them to be defeated by the combined armies of Moab, Ammon, and Amalek. Eglon, king of Moab, ruled over God's people for eighteen years until they once again repented.

This time the Lord sent a Benjamite named Ehud to deliver his people. Ehud assassinated Eglon in gruesome fashion at Gilgal, and then led the Israelites to a decisive victory over the Moabites by cutting off their retreat across the Jordan River.

This triumph led to eighty years of peace.

---

292. See Judges 2:20-3:4. The quote is from Judges 3:4.

Questions to ponder or discuss: Ehud attached a sword to his thigh, lied in order to get a private audience with Eglon, and then murdered the Moabite king in cold blood. Did Ehud's objective of freeing the Israelites from Moabite oppression justify the methods he used? When, if ever, does a worthy end justify wicked means used to accomplish it?

Chapter 57
Deborah the Prophetess
(Judges chapters 4 – 5)

Sometime after Ehud died, the Israelites again turned to evil. So God allowed them to be oppressed for twenty years by Jabin, a Canaanite king. He ruled from the city of Hazor, a stronghold north of the Sea of Galilee, in the territory of Naphtali. Jabin had a strong army, with 900 iron chariots—a powerful weapon the Israelites lacked.

Judges 5:6 hints at how onerous Jabin's rule must have been for the Israelites: "the highways were deserted, and travelers went by roundabout ways." People were too fearful to use normal routes of travel, probably because those routes were patrolled by Jabin's soldiers.

When God's people sought his help, he delivered his message through Deborah, who was both a judge and a prophetess. She summoned Barak son of Abinoam and instructed him to gather an army of 10,000 men to defeat Jabin.

Jabin's influence was probably limited to the northern portions of Palestine. This is a logical deduction from several facts: (1) Deborah judged in Ephraim and did not seem to be impacted by Jabin's oppression; (2) Deborah instructed Barak to draw his army from two northern tribes, Zebulun and Naphtali, whose territory was located west and north of the Sea of Galilee;[293] and (3) the ensuing battle occurred at the Kishon River, which is in northern Israel.

Barak agreed to follow Deborah's instructions only if she would accompany him. She consented, but warned him that this would result in him forfeiting the honor that would

---

293. Judges 4:6, 10; however, Judges 5:14-17 implies that some of the other tribes also sent troops.

otherwise be his, and that this honor would instead go to a woman. Barak probably thought Deborah was referring to herself.

Per Judges 5:21, the Kishon River flooded during the battle, rendering Jabin's chariots ineffective. As a result, the Lord gave Barak a decisive victory.

After the battle, Jabin's general, Sisera, fled for his life to the tent of Heber the Kenite. Heber's wife, Jael, took Sisera in, hid him, gave him something to drink—and then drove a tent peg through his skull as he slept. Thus, a woman, rather than Barak, received the honor of killing Sisera.

After this victory, the land had peace for another forty years.

Questions to ponder or discuss: Barak doubted Deborah's message until she was willing to place her own safety in jeopardy by accompanying him. Can you think of a time (or times) when someone else's faithful actions helped bolster your own faith? Now think of a time when you acted on your faith. Did it help inspire anyone else? Do you believe that faith can be contagious? Explain.

Chapter 58
Gideon Is Called By God
(Judges 6:1 – 6:32)

When the Israelites once more turned to idolatry and the evil it produced, the Lord allowed them to be oppressed by the Midianites for seven years. The Midianites lived east and southeast of the Dead Sea. These oppressors were not so much conquerors as nomadic raiders. Using domesticated camels, which permitted long-distance raids, the Midianites and their allies—the Amalekites and "the sons of the east"[294]—descended upon the Israelites periodically like a swarm of locusts, stealing their food and livestock.

As before, the Israelites cried to God for help. This time he sent them an unlikely deliverer: Gideon, from the tribe of Manasseh.

When we first meet Gideon, he is hardly the picture of courage. He is threshing wheat in a wine press. In those days, a wine press was essentially a hole dug into the ground and lined with stone—not unlike a small swimming pool. Gideon was threshing wheat in an empty wine press in order to hide what he was doing from the Midianites.

An angel appeared and hailed him, "The LORD is with you, O valiant warrior."[295] Gideon's reply can only be characterized as insolent and rude: he accused God of abandoning his people, and asked, "Where are all His miracles?"[296] It would not be the last time Gideon would test God's patience.

---

294. Judges 6:3
295. Judges 6:12
296. Judges 6:13

127

When the angel told him to deliver Israel from the Midianites, Gideon echoed Moses' reluctance: "How shall I deliver Israel?," pointing out that his youth and the insignificance of his family made him an unlikely candidate for such a calling.[297] But of course, God does not take "No" for an answer. So when Gideon requested a sign, the angel gave him one, producing fire from a rock to consume Gideon's offering of meat and bread. That prodded him to action.

Sneaking around at night for fear of his father and the townspeople, Gideon and ten of his servants destroyed his father's altar to the god Baal. Then he built an altar to God on top of it, burning a wooden idol as fuel for his own burnt offering. When the townspeople demanded that he be executed for this offense, his father unexpectedly came to his defense: "If [Baal] is a god, let him contend for himself, because someone has torn down his altar."[298]

Gideon escaped punishment for demolishing his father's idols, but he still had the Midianites to deal with. They soon assembled a huge army in the valley of Jezreel in central Palestine. Judges does not tell us whether this happened in response to what Gideon had done or was just another of many raids. But either way, Gideon's doubt would again be on full display, after which he would face a remarkable test of his faith in God.

Question to ponder or discuss: Gideon was certainly an unlikely deliverer. But God often chooses the weak and meek rather than the mighty. For example, he chose the Israelites rather than a powerful people like the Egyptians,

---

297. Judges 6:15

298. Judges 6:31

Chapter 58 – Gideon Is Called By God

Babylonians, or Romans, and he chose the shepherd boy David to become king of Israel. Why do you think he does that?

Chapter 59
A Sword For the Lord and For Gideon
(Judges 6:33 –7:25)

The Midianites and their allies mustered 135,000 warriors and camped in central Palestine, in the valley of Jezreel.[299] In response, Gideon was able to assemble an army of only 32,000 Israelites.

Not surprisingly, Gideon's faith wavered, so he decided to test the Lord to see "if You will deliver Israel through me, as You have spoken."[300]

Gideon set out a fleece of wool and asked the Lord to put dew only on the fleece and not on the surrounding ground. The Lord did so.

But Gideon was not satisfied. He probably worried that this could have been a coincidence. So he set out the fleece again the next day and asked the Lord to put dew on the surrounding ground while keeping the fleece dry.

I have long thought Gideon was fortunate that the Lord did not strike him dead for his audacity and lack of faith. Yet the Lord honored this request, too. Perhaps God was so patient because he had a supreme test of faith planned for Gideon.

With his army camped near the Midianites, God told Gideon that he had too many warriors, lest the Israelites think that the approaching victory was the result of their own efforts. So the Lord directed him to send home any warriors who were afraid. 22,000 left.

But the remaining 10,000 were still too many. So God tested them by how they drank water at a nearby spring.

---

299. Judges 6:33 and 8:10

300. Judges 6:36

Chapter 59 – A Sword For the Lord and For Gideon

Those who stayed upright and drank water with their hands so they could keep watch on their surroundings were allowed to remain, while those who were less cautious were sent home. The puny Israelite army dwindled to a mere 300.

Gideon must have doubted the Lord again, as any of us would have. So the Lord sent him secretly into the Midianite camp, where he heard one man say to another, "God has given Midian and all the camp into [Gideon's] hand."[301] Thus reassured, this "valiant warrior" returned to his men and prepared them for the unlikeliest of victories.

They armed themselves with trumpets[302] and concealed torches, but apparently no weapons.[303] Then they surrounded the Midianite camp at night, in three groups of 100 men. All at once they blew their trumpets, revealed their torches, and cried out, "A sword for the LORD and for Gideon!"[304] If God had not been faithful to his promise to give them victory, they would have been massacred.

God was faithful.

Surrounded by darkness, confusion, and Gideon's loud warriors, the Midianites and their allies panicked.[305] They fought each other, and many died, while others fled for their lives. Gideon summoned additional warriors from the

---

301. Judges 7:14

302. "Trumpet" in the Old Testament usually refers to the shofar (or shophar), which is a ram's horn.

303. Judges does not say that the Israelites took any weapons. If they did, they certainly did not have them in hand. Judges 7:20 says they held the torches in their left hands and the trumpets in their right hands, so their hands were full.

304. Judges 7:20

305. If the Midianites and their allies spoke different languages, this would have added to the confusion.

nearby tribes of Naphtali, Asher, Manasseh, and Ephraim to attack the fleeing Midianites.

Judges 8:10 tells us that only 15,000 of the 135,000 Midianites survived, led by their two kings, Zebah and Zalmunna—with Gideon and his 300 men in pursuit.

Questions to ponder or discuss: 300 vs. 135,000! Those seem like impossible odds. But God wanted those impossible odds so the Israelites could not doubt who was responsible for the victory. When was the last time you asked God to do the "impossible"? Why do you think we are often reluctant to pray those "impossible" prayers?

Chapter 60
Gideon's Terrible Mistake
(Judges 8:1 – 8:28)

After the incredible victory over the Midianites, Gideon pursued the remnants of the enemy army and their two kings, Zebah and Zalmunna, as they fled east of the Jordan River.

Gideon's men were tired and hungry, so they asked for food from the people of the town of Succoth, in the territory of the tribe of Gad. The city leaders refused. Probably fearing the still formidable Midianite army of 15,000 more than Gideon's 300 weary warriors, they sarcastically pointed out that Gideon had not yet captured the Midianite kings. When Gideon moved on to the town of Penuel, he and his men received a similar reception.

Gideon caught up with the enemy and launched a successful surprise attack, routing the Midianites and capturing their two kings, whom he later executed. He then returned to Succoth and Penuel, the two cities that had refused hospitality for him and his men. He punished the elders of Succoth by whipping them with branches from thorn bushes. The men of Penuel were even less fortunate, for Gideon destroyed their tower and killed the men of the city.

These victories brought forty years of peace, throughout the remainder of Gideon's lifetime.

Gideon demonstrated his devotion to God by refusing the Israelites' offer to make him king over Israel, saying, "The LORD shall rule over you."[306]

However, he made one terrible mistake. He asked each of the Israelites to give him a gold earring from the

---

306. Judges 8:23

133

plunder captured from the Midianites. Then he melted down the resulting seventy pounds of gold and formed it into a golden ephod, which became an object of idolatry for Gideon and the Israelites.

Questions to ponder or discuss: An ephod was part of the high priest's attire when serving in the Tabernacle.[307] Judges does not tell us how or why Gideon's golden ephod became an object of idolatry. Perhaps the ephod's allure was its beauty, or its value, or simply because it belonged to Gideon, who must have been a national hero. But how does a man who had seen so many miracles drift away from the true faith? What does that teach us? How is that a warning for us?

---

307. See Exodus 28:6-35.

Chapter 61
Abimelech's Treachery
(Judges 8:29 – 9:57)

Gideon (also known as Jerubbaal[308]) had many wives and seventy-two sons—including an illegitimate son named Abimelech. His mother was Gideon's concubine in the city of Shechem, one of the six cities of refuge. Shechem was centrally located in Palestine, west of the Jordan River. Joshua had gathered the Israelites there to address them shortly before he died.[309]

After Gideon's death, Israel relapsed into idolatry, which probably explains the wickedness that quickly followed.

Abimelech persuaded the leaders of Shechem to help him murder Gideon's other sons and make him king. Abimelech argued that they would be better off being ruled by him, a Shechemite like them, rather than by Gideon's seventy-one other sons. Perhaps the Shechemites feared a war for succession among Gideon's descendants. Or maybe they just liked the idea of one of their own being in power.

So Abimelech and the men of Shechem executed Gideon's sons—all except one, that is. Jotham, the youngest, escaped. He denounced his brothers' murderers and pronounced a curse upon them—that is, that Abimelech and the men of Shechem would destroy each other.

---

308. Chapter nine of Judges refers to Gideon as Jerubbaal—meaning "Let Baal contend against him"—a name his father gave Gideon after he destroyed the altar of Baal. See Judges 6:31-32.

309. Joshua 24:1-28

Judges 9:22 says that Abimelech "ruled over Israel" for three years, which is the first time Judges uses this language about one of the judges. (This of course contrasts with what Gideon said in Judges 8:23, as we noted in chapter sixty: "The LORD shall rule over you.")

The murders perpetrated by Abimelech and the Shechemites soon soured their relationship. Judges 9:23 says God sent an "evil spirit" between them. The Shechemites revolted against Abimelech's authority, led by Gaal, son of Ebed. Their revolt was short-lived, for Abimelech destroyed the Shechemites and their city, then "sowed it with salt"[310]— a common practice that was intended to make the land unsuitable for future cultivation.

After this he moved on to besiege the city of Thebez, which was probably Shechem's ally in this rebellion. There Abimelech met his own demise. Mortally wounded by a millstone thrown by a woman from a city tower, he ordered his armor bearer to slay him, lest it be said that a woman killed Abimelech.

Thus, "God repaid the wickedness of Abimelech" and the men of Shechem, "and the curse of Jotham the son of Gideon came upon them."[311]

Question to ponder or discuss: We like to think that evil-doers eventually get the punishment they deserve, and it was certainly so in the case of Abimelech and the men of Shechem. But how often do you think that really happens? Explain.

---

310. Judges 9:45

311. Judges 9:56-57

Chapter 62
Jephthah's Reckless Vow
(Judges chapters 10 – 11)

Two faithful judges ruled Palestine for forty-five years: Tola son of Puah, an Ephraimite, and Jair of Gilead, from the tribe of Gad.

After that, the Israelites again turned to idolatry by worshiping the many gods of the surrounding pagans. For eighteen years the Lord allowed them to be oppressed by the Philistines from the west[312] and the Ammonites from the east. The Ammonites coveted the land east of the Jordan River which the Israelites had taken from the Amorites.

This time when the Israelites asked God for deliverance, he refused: "Go and cry out to the gods which you have chosen; let them deliver you."[313] Yet when his people rid themselves of their idols and returned to serving the Lord, he relented and sent them Jephthah from Gilead.

Jephthah was the illegitimate son of his father (whose name was Gilead, like the city). His mother was a prostitute. When Jephthah grew up, his father's legitimate sons drove him away, and he became the leader of a gang of "worthless fellows."[314] He must have developed quite a reputation, because the elders of the city of Gilead made him their leader in return for his help in fighting the Ammonites.

As the day of battle approached, Jephthah made a rash vow to the Lord—in return for victory over the Ammonites, Jephthah pledged to offer as a burnt offering "whatev-

---

312. The Philistines lived along and near the Mediterranean coast of Israel.

313. Judges 10:14

314. Judges 11:2-3

er comes out of the doors of my house to meet me when I return."[315]

When Jephthah returned after a spectacular victory over the Ammonites, his daughter—his only child—ran to meet him. Although heartbroken, Jephthah carried out his vow two months later, sacrificing his only child.

Questions to ponder or discuss: God did not demand that Jephthah make a vow, nor did he command Jephthah to sacrifice his daughter. As we have observed before (chapter nine), the Lord had forbidden child sacrifice. Yet he did not stop Jephthah from carrying out his vow. Why do you think he didn't? Does God have a responsibility to save us from our own stupidity? Why or why not?

---

315. Judges 11:30-31

Chapter 63
Samson Enraged
(Judges chapters 12 – 15)

After Jephthah's death, three men—Ibzan, Elon, and Abdon—judged Israel for a total of twenty-five years. But the Israelites, as they so often did, again turned to evil, and God allowed the Philistines to oppress them for forty years.

Sometime during this forty years God prepared a deliverer who would "**begin to** deliver Israel from the hands of the Philistines."[316] An angel appeared to a Danite named Manoah and his wife, who was barren, to tell them that she would bear a child who was to become a Nazirite for life. What was a Nazirite?

Numbers 6:1-21 explains the Nazirite vow: an Israelite man or woman would take the vow for a certain period of time in order to dedicate themselves to the Lord. For the duration of the vow the person could not cut his hair, drink vinegar or anything alcoholic, consume grapes or grape juice, or go near a dead person.

As promised by the angel, Manoah's wife became pregnant and had a son, whom they named Samson. He would grow up to be strong enough to kill a lion with his bare hands. God began to use him from an early age.

In his youth Samson fell in love with one of the daughters of the Philistines. Judges 14:4 tells us that the Lord was behind this romance, "for He was seeking an occasion against the Philistines." That occasion came during Samson's wedding feast in his bride's hometown of Timnah.

---

316. Judges 13:5, emphasis added via boldface

Samson propounded a riddle involving honey in the body of the lion he had killed. He wagered thirty sets of clothing that the wedding guests would not be able to solve the riddle before the feast ended in seven days. He lost his bet when the guests persuaded his new wife to betray him and reveal the answer. Samson was so incensed at this treachery that he killed thirty Philistines in the city of Ashkelon and brought their clothes to pay off the bet. He then went home without his new wife.

Some months later Samson returned to claim his wife and found that her father had wed her to another man. Samson again lost his temper and burned the Philistines' crops and vineyards in revenge. The Philistines wanted to bring Samson to justice for this offense, and the men of Judah seemed only too happy to help if it saved them from Philistine retaliation. So they bound Samson and delivered him to the Philistines. But once in their hands, Samson burst his bonds and killed a thousand Philistines "with the jawbone of a donkey."[317]

This victory apparently kept the Philistines at bay for twenty years, for that is how long Samson judged Israel.[318]

Questions to ponder or discuss: God selected Samson to be a Nazirite before he was born, and then used him to help the Israelites escape Philistine oppression for a time. Like Mary, the mother of Jesus, Samson seems to have had little or no choice of his own in the matter. Does that seem

---

317. Judges 15:14-16. Personally, I wonder if there isn't more to this story, since it's hard to imagine one man single-handedly killing 1,000 enemies at one time, no matter how strong he is. Perhaps Samson led an uprising or an ambush, and gets the credit because he was the leader—just as we say that General Grant captured 29,000 Confederate soldiers in the battle of Vicksburg even though he obviously had help.

318. Judges 15:20

fair to you? Would you want to be used by God if you couldn't choose to do otherwise? Why or why not?

Chapter 64
Samson and Delilah
(Judges chapter 16)

I don't know if Samson was a fool, or—like many men—he was simply a fool when he was around women. In any event, he was a poor judge of the female of the species. His first wife betrayed him, which lost him a bet, but his next misjudgment about a woman would cost him his life.

He fell in love with a woman named Delilah, whom the Philistines bribed to help them capture Samson. To do so, she had to discover the secret of his incredible strength— and thus, how he could be overcome.

The first time she asked, Samson wisely lied, telling her that binding him "with seven fresh cords that have not been dried" would render him helpless.[319] But when she tried tying him up in that manner and then called out, "The Philistines are upon you, Samson!," he easily broke free.[320]

This scenario was repeated two more times—once with "new ropes which have not been used"[321] and then by weaving his hair into a loom—and each time when she bound him according to his directions he quickly broke free.

After being lied to those three times, Delilah played dirty: she accused Samson of not loving her, then nagged him constantly to tell her his secret.[322]

At this point I'm reminded of the famous adage, "Fool me once, shame on you. Fool me twice, shame on me."

---

319. Judges 16:7

320. Judges 16:8-9

321. Judges 16:11-12

322. Judges 16:15-16

Chapter 64 – Samson and Delilah

Delilah had tried to bind Samson three times without success, yet he didn't seem to suspect a thing. He must have been one love-sick puppy not to realize that she could not be trusted.

She finally wore him down and he told her the truth—that he was a Nazirite, and that he would lose his strength if his hair was cut. Delilah reported this information to the Philistines.

As Samson slept, a Philistine shaved his head, enabling his enemies to capture him, blind him, and imprison him in the Philistine city of Gaza. Judges 16:19 explains that breaking the Nazirite vow by cutting his hair caused the Lord to depart from him.

Sometime later,[323] the Philistine nobility held a celebration for their god Dagon, to whom they credited their victory. In the midst of this party, they brought Samson up from prison to "amuse" them.[324] While they celebrated, Samson asked God to give him his strength one last time—and then broke the pillars that supported the structure, killing himself and 3,000 Philistines.

Questions to ponder or discuss: Does it trouble you that Samson prayed for the strength to kill? Does it trouble you that God apparently granted his prayer (although Judges does not explicitly say so)? Why or why not?

---

323. Judges does not tell us how much later this occurred. Judges 16:22 ("the hair of his head began to grow again") may imply that Samson's hair had regrown by then, although that is not specifically stated.

324. Judges 16:25

Chapter 65
The Corrupting of the Danites
(Judges chapters 17 – 18)

Chapter seventeen of Judges tells the strange story of Micah,[325] a man within the territory of Ephraim whose family turned to idolatry. He later hired a Levite from Bethlehem to be his priest. Micah, it seems, wanted to cover all his religious bases.

As we have noted before (chapter fifty-five), the tribe of Dan failed to conquer the territory allotted to them.[326] So they sent five spies to search for a suitable alternative. The spies traveled through Ephraim and recognized Micah's Levite, who assured them that their mission "has the LORD's approval."[327] Subsequent events make me doubt that what the Levite said was true, but he probably told them what they wanted to hear.

The Danite spies eventually came to the city of Laish, about twenty-five miles north of the Sea of Galilee. The land around Laish was spacious and rich, and the people were isolated and peaceful. So the spies returned and urged the Danites to go at once and seize the land. Six-hundred warriors responded, taking their families and possessions with them.

Along the way to Laish, the Danites stole Micah's idols and convinced the Levite to accompany them and become their priest. When Micah and his neighbors discovered the theft, they set out in pursuit, but backed down when the Danites threatened to kill them.

---

325. This was not Micah the prophet, the subject of the Book of Micah.

326. See Judges 1:34

327. Judges 18:6

Chapter 65 – The Corrupting of the Danites

The Danites reached Laish, killed its people, and burned the city. Then they rebuilt it and named it Dan.

After King Solomon's kingdom split, Jeroboam, king of the northern kingdom of Israel, made Dan one of two centers of idolatrous worship there.[328] That began the northern kingdom's downward spiral into idolatry and evil.

Questions to ponder or discuss: Judges 17:6 says, "In those days there was no king in Israel; every man did what was right in his own eyes," a sentiment echoed elsewhere in Judges.[329] This tells us that Judges was probably written sometime after Israel acquired a king. But it also sounds like the author is trying to use the lack of a king as an excuse for the conduct of the Danites (as well as what follows in chapters nineteen through twenty-one). Why do you think we make excuses for our bad behavior? What are some common excuses we use?[330]

---

328. See 1 Kings 12:25-33 and 2 Chronicles 11:14-15

329. Judges 18:1, 19:1, 21:25

330. For example: "Everybody does it." Or "He (or she) made me do it."

Chapter 66
Civil War
(Judges chapters 19 – 20)

Chapters nineteen and twenty of the book of Judges describe a civil war that occurred during the high priesthood of Phinehas, Eleazar's son. Since Eleazar was a contemporary of Joshua,[331] this event probably occurred close in time to the judgeship of Othniel, Israel's first judge.

The war arose over the mistreatment of a Levite's concubine within the territory of the tribe of Benjamin. While traveling home to Ephraim, the Levite and his concubine stopped in the city of Gibeah,[332] where they were given shelter and hospitality by an old man who lived there. But in a scene reminiscent of Sodom, some local thugs demanded that they be allowed to have sexual relations with the Levite. As in Sodom, this was a gross violation of Middle Eastern hospitality traditions.

In what can only be described as a selfish and heartless act, the Levite instead gave them his concubine, whom they raped and abused all night. The next morning she was dead.

The callousness of the old man and the Levite toward women is striking. The old man offered his own virgin daughter as well as the Levite's concubine to the men of Gibeah if they would leave the man alone. The Levite, after delivering his concubine to the men for them to abuse, slept peacefully until morning. Then upon finding her in the

---

331. Eleazar's death is mentioned in Joshua 24:33.

332. Gibeah was located a few miles north of Jerusalem.

doorway, he seemed unconcerned about her well-being, saying simply, "Get up and let us go," before realizing that she was dead.[333]

The Levite took her body back home and cut it into twelve pieces, which he sent throughout Israel. The Israelites were so incensed they demanded that the Benjamites hand over the men responsible to be executed. But the men of Benjamin refused and prepared for war.

The Benjamites, although badly outnumbered, managed to win the first two battles against the rest of Israel. But in the third battle the Israelites used Joshua's tactics in his fight against the city of Ai, laying an ambush to lure the Benjamites away from Gibeah in order to surround and destroy them.

Questions to ponder or discuss: Why do you think the Benjamites chose to go to war rather than hand over the offenders for execution? Where would you draw the line between devotion to what you know to be right vs. loyalty to relatives?

---

333. Judges 19:28

Chapter 67

Benjamin Saved

(Judges chapter 21)

After their defeat at Gibeah, not many young men from the tribe of Benjamin remained. Judges 20:46-47 tells us that only 600 out of more than 25,000 Benjamite warriors survived the battle.

Judges 21 implies that the tribe of Benjamin was close to extinction, which may be hyperbole. Yet the tribe had been severely weakened, perhaps to the point that they could no longer defend themselves against—much less conquer—the remaining Canaanites within their territory. (Recall that this occurred at about the time Othniel was judging Israel, which was not long after Joshua had defeated the Canaanite armies, so pockets of resistance remained in the land.)

To make matters worse, the Israelites had all taken an oath prior to the battle not to give any of their daughters to the Benjamites as wives.[334] Now they faced a dilemma: how to repopulate Benjamin without violating their oath.

A partial solution was found in Jabesh-gilead, the one city which had not gone to war against Benjamin. (Jabesh-gilead was located east of the Jordan River.) The Israelites sent 12,000 warriors to destroy the city and its inhabitants,[335]

---

334. Judges 21:1. The implication of this, as well as Judges 20:48, is that the Israelites in their zeal had slaughtered all of the Benjamite women and children.

335. As we will see in chapter seventy-four, the city of Jabesh-gilead existed at the time of King Saul. So either the city was not completely destroyed, or it was rebuilt.

except for 400 young virgin women who were brought back as wives for the Benjamites.

But more wives were needed. So the Israelites told the men of Benjamin to steal wives from among the daughters of Shiloh[336] during the annual feast for the Lord. In this way, the men of Shiloh would not violate their oath, since they did not "give" their daughters to the Benjamites.

Questions to ponder or discuss: What was the purpose of the Israelites' oath to deny their daughters to the Benjamites?

At the time of their oath, the Israelites must have believed it was the right thing to do, but in retrospect they regretted it because it could have meant the extinction of one of the tribes of Israel. Has there been a time when you did something you believed was the right thing, but your actions had unintended consequences that you regretted? How did you react to those unintended consequences?

---

336. Shiloh was located about twenty-seven miles north of Jerusalem, just west of today's Shiloh (or Shilo), Israel.

Chapter 68
Ruth and Naomi
(Ruth chapter 1)

Ruth 1:16-17: "Do not urge me to leave you or turn back from following you; for where you go, I will go, and where you lodge, I will lodge. Your people shall be my people, and your God, my God. Where you die, I will die, and there I will be buried. Thus may the LORD do to me, and worse, if anything but death parts you and me."

Although these beautiful words of loyalty and devotion have been used in many wedding ceremonies, including my own, they were originally spoken by a daughter-in-law to her mother-in-law.

Ruth, the daughter-in-law, was a Moabite, a descendant of Abraham's nephew, Lot.

Naomi, the mother-in-law, was from Israel. She had married a man from Bethlehem, Elimelech, and they had two sons: Mahlon and Chilion. During a terrible famine in Israel, Elimelech moved Naomi and their two sons to Moab, and there he met an untimely death, leaving Naomi a widow.

Each of the two sons took a Moabite wife—Chilion married Orpah, and Mahlon married Ruth.[337] But after Naomi had been in Moab for about ten years both of the sons died. With her husband and sons dead, Naomi decided to return to Israel. Orpah stayed in Moab in the hope of landing another husband from among her people, but Ruth refused to be separated from Naomi. Those wonderful words in Ruth 1:16-17 convinced Naomi to let Ruth accompany her.

The two of them journeyed to Bethlehem, where

---

337. Ruth 4:10

Naomi gave herself a new name. Naomi means "pleasant." But she renamed herself Mara, meaning "bitter," because "the Almighty has dealt very bitterly with me. I went out full, but the LORD has brought me back empty."[338]

Questions to ponder or discuss: Naomi believed that God was responsible for her misfortune. Do you believe God inflicts calamities and adversity on people? Why or why not? How does Luke 13:1-5[339] impact your answer?

---

338. Ruth 1:20-21

339. In Luke 13:1-5, Jesus challenges the idea that some people who had lost their lives had suffered that fate because they were morally worse than the rest of society.

Chapter 69
Ruth and Boaz
(Ruth chapters 2 – 4)

Ruth and Naomi arrived in Bethlehem at the beginning of the barley harvest.[340] This was well-timed, because it kept them from starving to death.

Israel in the eleventh century B.C. had no social security to take care of widows like Naomi and Ruth. As a general rule, women depended upon their fathers, their husbands, or their children to take care of them. Ruth and Naomi had no one.

Fortunately, Leviticus 19:9-10 mandated that any grain or fruit which the reapers missed during the harvest be left for the poor. So Ruth followed the reapers and picked up the gleanings from the harvest. The field she chose happened to belong to Boaz, a relative of Naomi's deceased husband, Elimelech. Boaz was impressed with Ruth's kindness and devotion to Naomi. So he treated her generously, giving her food and water, and arranging for her to find abundant gleanings in his fields throughout the harvest season.

After the harvest, and at Naomi's suggestion, Ruth approached Boaz as he slept on the floor where he had been threshing wheat. There she "came secretly, and uncovered his feet and lay down."[341] Some have contended that this language implies consensual sexual relations, but this seems unlikely in view of Ruth 3:8, which says Boaz was "startled" to find her there when he suddenly awoke, and Ruth 3:11, where Boaz says that Ruth was well known as "a woman of excellence."

---

340. Ruth 1:22
341. Ruth 3:7

Even if all she did was lay down near him, her conduct was very risqué for that time and culture. She was clearly flirting and making known her willingness to become his wife. Boaz was flattered, because Ruth was significantly younger than he was. But one obstacle remained.

Under the Law, if a man died childless, his brother had a duty to marry the man's widow and have a child with her.[342] That child would then take the name of the deceased "so that his name will not be blotted out from Israel."[343] When the child grew up, he would inherit the land which had belonged to his deceased "father." If the dead man had no brother to perform this duty, the Book of Ruth implies that the right and responsibility fell to the man's closest living relative.[344]

Ruth's deceased husband, Mahlon, had a closer relation than Boaz. That relative was willing to purchase the land which had belonged to Mahlon, thus ensuring that it remained within the tribe of Judah. However, he was not willing to marry Ruth and give Mahlon an heir—for then the land which he had agreed to purchase would have been inherited by Ruth's child rather than his own children. So the relative surrendered his redemption rights to Boaz, who eagerly married Ruth.

Ruth and Boaz soon had a son named Obed, who would become the father of Jesse and the grandfather of King David. Thus, Ruth and Boaz were the great-grandparents of Israel's greatest king.

Questions to ponder or discuss: What do you think would have happened if Ruth had remained in Moab? How

---

342. Deuteronomy 25:5-6

343. Deuteronomy 25:6

344. See Ruth 3:12-13.

has God caused events in your life to lead you to where, what, and who you are today?

Chapter 70
Samuel and Eli
(1 Samuel 1:1 – 3:18)

Samuel was the son of Elkanah, a Levite living in the territory of Ephraim.[345] Elkanah had two wives: Hannah, who seemed unable to have children, and Peninnah.[346]

Because children served as additional workers in the field and security in a parent's old age, a woman who could not have children was either pitied or scorned in those days.[347] Nevertheless, Hannah was Elkanah's favorite, just as the long-barren Rachel had been Jacob's favorite.

Hannah prayed for a son, vowing to give him to the Lord if God would grant her prayer.[348] He did, and she gave birth to Samuel. After Samuel was weaned, Hannah took him to the tabernacle in Shiloh and gave the boy to Eli the priest as an apprentice. Hannah would go on to have five more children, while Samuel grew up in Shiloh under Eli's tutelage.

One evening when the boy was serving in the tabernacle, he heard a voice calling his name, so he presented himself to Eli. But Eli had not called him. This happened twice more before the priest realized that Samuel was being called by the Lord. Eli instructed the boy to respond the next time by saying, "Speak, LORD, for Your servant is listen-

---

345. Compare 1 Samuel 1:1 and 1 Chronicles 6:33-38.

346. Elkanah may have taken a second wife when he decided that Hannah could not give him children.

347. See, for example, 1 Samuel 1:6.

348. See 1 Samuel 1:10-11. Per 1 Samuel 1:11, part of Hannah's vow was that "a razor shall never come on his head." This may indicate that Samuel was a Nazirite like Samson.

ing."[349] Samuel did so and the Lord told him that he would soon execute judgment upon Eli's two sons, Hophni and Phinehas, "because his sons brought a curse on themselves and he [Eli] did not rebuke them."[350]

Like their father, Hophni and Phinehas were priests, but they were "worthless men"[351] who "despised the offering of the LORD."[352] 1 Samuel 2:12-17 explains that they consumed more of the offerings than merely the priests' portion, and seized the raw meat for themselves before the blood had been drained and the fat burned. [353] In addition, Hophni and Phinehas "lay with the women who served at the doorway of the tent of meeting."[354]

When Samuel told Eli what the Lord had said, he accepted it gracefully: "It is the LORD; let Him do what seems good to Him."[355] The prophecy would be fulfilled a few years later, at the Battle of Ebenezer.

---

349. 1 Samuel 3:9

350. 1 Samuel 3:13

351. 1 Samuel 2:12

352. 1 Samuel 2:17

353. The Law forbid the consumption of blood and fat. (See Leviticus 3:16-17, 7:23-27, and 17:10-14.) Nothing from a burnt offering could be eaten because it was to be completely burned up (Leviticus 1:9, 1:13), except for the skin, which belonged to the priest (Leviticus 7:8). The priests could eat a portion of all other offerings. See, for example: Leviticus 7:31-34 (peace offering); Leviticus 7:6-7 (guilt offering); Leviticus 6:24-29 (sin offering); Leviticus 6:18 (grain offering); Numbers 18:19 and Deuteronomy 18:3-4 (offerings belong to the priests, except those portions which are required to be burned up).

354. 1 Samuel 2:22

355. 1 Samuel 3:18

Questions to ponder or discuss: Although 1 Samuel 3:13 says Eli failed to rebuke his sons, 1 Samuel 2:23-25 explains that he did warn them to stop their wickedness, but the warning was ineffectual. Perhaps the warning was not tough enough or simply came too late, when Eli was "very old."[356] Why do parents sometimes fail to properly discipline their children? Why—and how—does God discipline us as his children?

---

356. 1 Samuel 2:22

Chapter 71
Disaster at Ebenezer
(1 Samuel 3:19 –4:22)

Palestine derives its name from the Philistines, who were from Caphtor.[357] Biblical scholars believe Caphtor refers to Crete, a large island in the eastern Mediterranean Sea. The Philistines resided in western Palestine, along and near the Mediterranean coast.

The Israelites had been battling the Philistines since at least the time of Samson (and perhaps Jephthah). When Samuel was grown and Eli was ninety-eight years old, the Israelites fought the Philistines at Ebenezer. The Israelites were defeated and 4,000 Israelite soldiers lost their lives.

The Israelites decided they needed God's presence to help them win the next encounter, so they went to Shiloh and retrieved the Ark of the Covenant, which they carried with them into battle.

They lost again.

This defeat was worse than before. 30,000 Israelites died, including Eli's two incorrigible sons, Hophni and Phinehas. In addition, the Philistines captured the Ark.

A Benjamite carried word of the defeat back to Shiloh—and Eli. When he learned that the Ark had been captured, he fell backward and broke his neck, killing him. His time as judge over Israel ended after forty years.

But the tragedy for his family continued. Phinehas' wife went into labor when she heard the news about the defeat, the Ark, and the deaths of her husband, brother-in-law, and father-in-law. After giving birth to a boy named Ichabod, she too died.

---

357. See Amos 9:7, Jeremiah 47:4, and Deuteronomy 2:23.

Meanwhile, the Philistines carried the Ark back to Ashdod, one of the five major cities of the Philistines.[358] There they set it in the temple of their god, Dagon.[359]

Questions to ponder or discuss: The Israelites must have believed that God would never allow the Ark to be lost, and thus having the symbol of God's presence with them would ensure victory. What did they do wrong? What should they have done instead? Can we ever force God to do our bidding? Explain.

---

358. The other four major Philistine cities were Gaza, Ashkelon, Gath, and Ekron. See 1 Samuel 6:17.

359. 1 Samuel 5:1-2

Chapter 72
God vs. the Philistines
(1 Samuel 5:1 –7:2)

As we saw in chapter seventy-one, the Philistines captured the Ark of the Covenant in the battle at Ebenezer. They would keep it for about seven months.[360]

First they brought it to Ashdod, where they placed it beside a statue of their god, Dagon. The next morning, Dagon's statue had fallen over. The Philistines uprighted it, but the next morning the statue had fallen over again, and this time it had been decapitated and the palms of its hands cut off. In addition, the Lord plagued the people of the city with mice and "tumors," which may refer to hemorrhoids.[361]

The leaders of Ashdod realized they needed to rid themselves of the Ark. So they consulted with the leaders of the other four major Philistine cities—Gath, Gaza, Ashkelon, and Ekron—and decided to send the Ark to Gath.

The people of Gath suffered the same plagues as Ashdod. So they sent the Ark to Ekron, whose people panicked at the prospect of having the Ark in their midst.

The Philistine leaders, after consultation with their religious leaders, decided to send the Ark back to Israel with a "guilt offering" of gold in the shape of five tumors and five mice.[362] They put the Ark and the guilt offering on a cart pulled by two cows that were still producing milk and had never been yoked. The fact that they were producing milk implies that they had recently given birth and would want to

---

360. 1 Samuel 6:1

361. 1 Samuel 6:4-5

362. 1 Samuel 6:3-5

return to their nursing calves. Instead, the cows pulled the cart toward Israel, proving that God had been the cause of the Philistines' misfortune. The cows headed straight for the town of Beth-shemesh, in Israel.

There the people acted foolishly. They killed the cows as a burnt offering to the Lord. Such offerings were supposed to be made only by the priests and only at the Tabernacle. Worse, they looked inside the Ark. Only the priests were allowed to even see the holy objects that were normally kept inside the Tabernacle, including the Ark, and no one was allowed to touch it—much less look inside.[363]

As a result, the Lord killed seventy (some manuscripts say 50,070) men of Beth-shemesh. After that, the men of Kiriath-jearim took custody of the Ark. It would remain there for twenty years.

Questions to ponder or discuss: The story of God's treatment of the people of Beth-shemesh provides another example of the Lord punishing people for their insolence and lack of reverence—just as he did with the rebellious followers of Korah and the Israelites who complained about manna. How is this similar to what Paul said about the Corinthians' disrespect for the Lord's Supper in 1 Corinthians 11:17-34? Why would God punish people who display such an attitude toward him?

---

363. Exodus 25:12-15 and Numbers 4:15-20

Chapter 73
Victory Over the Philistines
(1 Samuel 7:3 – 7:15)

Samuel promised the Israelites that if they would quit worshiping idols, return to the Lord, and worship him alone, then God would deliver them from the Philistines. Surprisingly, the Israelites did exactly that.

Samuel called the people of Israel to gather at Mizpah to fast, pray, and confess that "We have sinned against the LORD."[364] Mizpah had been the Israelites' assembly point when Jephthah led them against the Ammonites,[365] and again when the Israelites went to war against the Benjamites.[366]

Although this was a religious assembly, the Philistines must have regarded it as a step toward rebellion. They prepared for war. At the urging of the people, who were terrified, Samuel presented a burnt offering to the Lord and prayed for him to protect his people.

The Lord delivered.

When the Philistine army approached the Israelites, God "thundered with a great thunder on that day against the Philistines and confused them, so that they were routed before Israel."[367] This sounds like God sent a severe thunderstorm or hailstorm, which may have frightened the Philistines—especially after the incident with the Ark. Large hailstones could have injured or killed some of the enemy

---

364. 1 Samuel 7:5-6

365. Judges 10:17

366. Judges 20:1

367. 1 Samuel 7:10

soldiers, and muddy ground may have negated many of the Philistine's military advantages. In any event, Israel achieved a great victory. She regained all of the territory which the Philistines had taken and they did not bother the Israelites again until after Saul had become king.

Samuel commemorated the victory by setting up a stone monument and naming it Ebenezer—perhaps in an effort to remove the emotional stench of Israel's earlier defeat.

Samuel would go on to judge Israel "all the days of his life,"[368] although he may have shared this responsibility with Saul after he became king (depending on exactly what the Israelites considered to be the duties of a "judge").

Questions to ponder or discuss: Why do we construct monuments and statues? What, if anything, do they have to do with our desire for immortality?

---

368. 1 Samuel 7:15

Chapter 74
The Israelites Get a King
(1 Samuel 7:16 – 8:22)

When Samuel was judging Israel, he lived in Ramah, but every year he traveled to the city centers of Bethel, Gilgal, and Mizpah to hear disputes. All of these cities were in central Israel, not far from Shiloh, where the tabernacle normally resided.[369]

When Samuel grew old, he appointed his sons, Joel and Abijah, as judges in Beersheba, in southern Israel. Perhaps Samuel did this to help share the burden or to meet a need in the south that he could no longer handle himself. Whatever the reason, the decision was unfortunate. Joel and Abijah were corrupt and greedy. They took bribes and used their positions to enrich themselves instead of impartially administering justice.[370]

At about the same time, Israel faced invasion by the Ammonites, who besieged Jabesh-gilead in northern Israel, east of the Jordan River.[371]

Unhappy with Samuel's sons, and fearing the Ammonites, the elders of Israel asked Samuel to "appoint a king for us to judge us like all the nations."[372] Samuel felt insulted, for he believed the people were rejecting him as their judge. When he prayed, the Lord told him to give the people their king, but to also tell them what having a king would mean.

---

369. We have noted previously that the tabernacle usually resided at Shiloh. See chapters sixty-seven, seventy, and seventy-one.

370. 1 Samuel 8:3

371. 1 Samuel 11:1-2 and 12:12. Jabesh-Gilead was about twenty miles south of the Sea of Galilee and near the Jordan River.

372. 1 Samuel 8:5 and 12:12

Chapter 74 – The Israelites Get a King

Samuel warned them that a king would take their sons for his army, their daughters to be his servants, and a portion of their crops and possessions to pay for his lifestyle. Samuel also told them the Lord would not listen to their future complaints about their king. Despite these warnings, the people insisted on receiving a king, "that we also may be like all the nations, that our king may judge us and go out before us and fight our battles."[373]

The Lord chose Saul as king—a tall, handsome man from the tribe of Benjamin.[374]

Questions to ponder or discuss: When Samuel prayed, the Lord told him: "they have not rejected you, but they have rejected Me from being king over them."[375] In chapter twelve of 1 Samuel, Samuel chastises the people because they asked for a king. Why was their request "evil," as it is called in 1 Samuel 12:19-20? Is fear of the future indicative of a weakness in our faith? Why or why not? What should we do when we feel overwhelmed by our problems?

---

373. 1 Samuel 8:20

374. 1 Samuel 9:1-2, 9:15-17, and 10:20-23

375. 1 Samuel 8:7

Chapter 75
King Saul
(1 Samuel chapters 9 – 10)

Before he was anointed as king, Saul described himself as "a Benjamite, of the smallest of the tribes of Israel, and my family the least of all the families of the tribe of Benjamin."[376] The first is probably true, for the Benjamites had been decimated during the civil war that almost destroyed them. Choosing a king from the smallest and weakest of the twelve tribes may have avoided arousing jealousy and rivalry among the other tribes.

But Saul's claim about his family does not quite ring true, because his family owned donkeys, a prized animal at that time, indicating at least moderate wealth.[377]

Those donkeys brought Saul and Samuel together. The animals wandered away, and Saul's father, Kish, sent Saul in search of them. That search eventually led him to Samuel—who was well known as a prophet—in the hope that he would know where the donkeys were. Samuel told Saul that the animals were safe, and then secretly anointed him as king over Israel.

Samuel also told Saul that he would soon receive the "Spirit of the LORD," leading him to prophesy "and be changed into another man"—all of which happened.[378]

Finally, Samuel told Saul to wait at Gilgal for seven days until Samuel came down to offer burnt offerings and

---

376. 1 Samuel 9:21

377. In addition, 1 Samuel 9:1 says that Saul's father was "a mighty man of valor." The word for "valor" can also be translated as "wealth" or "influence."

378. 1 Samuel 10:6 and 10:9-13

peace offerings. As we shall see, this simple instruction—or one like it—would be Saul's undoing.

To make Saul's selection as king official, Samuel called for a meeting of the Israelites at Mizpah. There he cast lots to determine the new king. Casting lots was a random selection method. The Israelites believed that God would manipulate the lots to lead them to his choice.[379]

The casting of lots selected the tribe of Benjamin, then Saul's family, and finally Saul himself, who was proclaimed king of Israel.

Questions to ponder or discuss: When Saul was chosen as king, the people found him "hiding himself by the baggage."[380] Probably for this reason, some were skeptical of his selection as king, saying to themselves, "How can this one deliver us?"[381] When have you seen somebody accomplish things beyond your expectations? Why do we so often judge people by our first impression of them?

---

379. See, for example, Joshua 7:14-21, where lots were used to detect Achan's sin after the battle of Jericho.

380. 1 Samuel 10:22

381. 1 Samuel 10:27

Chapter 76
King Saul Proves Himself
(1 Samuel chapter 11)

As we noted in chapter seventy-four, one of the reasons the Israelites wanted a king was to lead them into battle against the Ammonites, who had invaded the territory east of the Jordan River and besieged the city of Jabesh-gilead. When the leaders of the city sued for peace, the Ammonite leader, Nahash, demanded that he be allowed to gouge out each person's right eye. This would impede their future prowess in battle—not only would they forfeit their depth perception, but their vision would be further impaired because the remaining left eye would often be blocked by a man's shield (a right-handed man would hold the shield in his left hand, and a sword or spear in his right). Such savagery is consistent with what Amos 1:13 says about the Ammonites: "they ripped open the pregnant women of Gilead."

Understandably reluctant to submit to this condition, the city leaders played for time while they sent out an urgent appeal for help throughout Israel. When the appeal reached Saul in Gibeah, he took swift action. He summoned all of Israel to come to the aid of Jabesh-gilead, threatening them with destruction if they ignored the call. All responded.

1 Samuel 11:8 tells us that 300,000 men came from Israel and 30,000 from Judah.

Saul sent word to Jabesh-gilead that help was on the way, no doubt to ensure that they would not surrender before the army could reach them.

Dividing his army into three groups and attacking in the early morning hours—mimicking Gideon's strategy of surrounding and surprising the enemy—Saul routed the

Ammonites. Then he showed his mercy by refusing to punish the Israelites who had questioned his leadership when he was anointed as king.

At Samuel's urging, the Israelites traveled to Gilgal, where they once again proclaimed Saul king and celebrated with peace offerings to the Lord.

Questions to ponder or discuss: Samuel led the people to Gilgal—which had been the site of the Israelite camp when they invaded Canaan—instead of to Shiloh where the tabernacle was usually set up. [382] Perhaps this indicates that Samuel regarded the anointing of a king as a political act rather than a religious event. Do you agree with this interpretation? Why or why not?

What should be the relationship between religion and government? Or between religion and politics?

---

382. Here and in chapter seventy-eight, below, we see offerings being made at Gilgal rather than at Shiloh, apparently with Samuel's approval. It is possible that the Israelites moved the Tabernacle to Gilgal for these occasions.

Chapter 77
How Long Did King Saul Reign?
(1 Samuel 13:1)

We are told in two places in the Bible that King Saul ruled Israel for about forty years. 1 Samuel 13:1 says he was thirty years old when his reign began, and that he was king for forty-two years. Acts 13:21 comes from Paul's sermon in the synagogue at Pisidian Antioch, in which he says: "Then they asked for a king, and God gave them Saul . . . for forty years." Despite these two verses, his reign was probably much shorter.

The statement in 1 Samuel 13:1 is suspect, because it is based on the Septuagint—the Greek translation of the Hebrew Old Testament that was widely used and quoted during Jesus' time. Ancient Hebrew manuscripts do not say "forty-two years," but "two years." Scholars believe the number that preceded "two" somehow got omitted, so Saul could have been king for twelve years, twenty-two years, thirty-two years, etc.

Paul's statement in Acts 13:21 is also based on the Septuagint, which was commonly used in the Greek-speaking eastern Roman Empire. This doesn't mean that the Bible is inaccurate—it truthfully and correctly records what Paul said. But that doesn't mean that what Paul said was historically accurate.

So why do scholars think Saul's reign was shorter than forty years? We find our first clue by comparing 1 Samuel 7:1-2 with 2 Samuel 6:2 and 1 Chronicles 13:5-6. After the Philistines returned the Ark of the Covenant which they had captured in the battle at Ebenezer, 1 Samuel 7:1-2 says that it remained in Kiriath-jearim for twenty years—

until King David retrieved it, per 2 Samuel 6:2 and 1 Chronicles 13:5-6. The battle of Ebenezer took place before Saul became king, when Eli was still alive. David retrieved the Ark after he had already been king over Judah for seven years, per 2 Samuel 5:1-5. So that leaves no more than about thirteen years for Saul to be king.

We find another clue in 1 Kings 6:1, which says that King Solomon (David's son and successor as king) began to build the temple in the fourth year of his reign, 480 years after the Exodus. If we add up the forty years before entering Canaan, the roughly 390 years encompassed by the chronology in the book of Judges, and David's forty years as king, per 2 Samuel 5:4—a total of 470 years—that leaves little time for Saul's reign.

Even if Judges' chronology is somewhat inflated (which it undoubtedly is), we still have not accounted for the time period between the capture of Jericho and the death of Joshua, after which a "new generation" arose.

Finally, we know that Samuel was already old when he anointed Saul as king, yet Samuel also anointed Saul's successor, David.[383] Samuel must have lived a very long time indeed if Saul ruled for forty years.

Questions to ponder or discuss: Assuming Paul was mistaken about the length of Saul's reign, how does that impact your view of Paul's preaching and his letters, if at all? Can the Biblical authors be fallible and still be telling the truth? Does the Bible have to be completely mistake-free to be true—or to be God's word? Explain.

---

383. 1 Samuel 16:13

Chapter 78
King Saul's First Big Blunder
(1 Samuel 13:2 – 13:14)

The separation of church and state is not something America invented. It dates back at least to the time of Samuel the priest-prophet and King Saul.

Saul had an army of 3,000 men, and placed 1,000 of them under the command of his son, Jonathan, at Gibeah. Saul and the other 2,000 men were north of there, in and near Michmash, about nine miles north of Jerusalem.

Jonathan attacked a Philistine garrison that was at Geba, within the territory of Benjamin. The Philistines naturally regarded this as an act of war and mobilized 30,000 chariots and 6,000 cavalrymen.[384] As the Philistine army approached Michmash, Saul retreated to Gilgal and summoned Israel to meet this new threat.[385]

By pre-arrangement Saul was to wait seven days in Gilgal until Samuel arrived to offer sacrifices to the Lord before battle. 1 Samuel 10:8 mentions a similar pre-arrangement that occurred shortly before Saul's commissioning as king and before his victory over the Ammonites. So perhaps this was their customary practice, to give Samuel time to travel from his home in Ramah to Gilgal.

---

384. 1 Samuel 13:5. In addition, the Philistines used superior iron weapons, whereas the Israelites had bronze. See 1 Samuel 13:19-22.

385. 1 Samuel 13:4-7. With Saul waiting in Gilgal, the Philistines sent out raiding parties against three towns: Ophrah, Beth-horon, and Zeboim. (1 Samuel 13:17-18) All were within the territory of Saul's tribe of Benjamin. (Joshua 18:13 and 18:23, and Nehemiah 11:34) The purpose of these raids was probably to try to force Saul to do battle.

Chapter 78 – King Saul's First Big Blunder

The seven days passed. As the people panicked and Saul's army deserted,[386] he decided he could wait no longer. He offered the burnt offering himself—which only a priest was permitted to do.[387] Thus, King Saul, the civil authority, infringed on the religious authority of Samuel the priest. Saul's actions angered both Samuel and God.

Saul, when Samuel confronted him, blamed everyone but himself: Samuel was late, the Philistines were bearing down, and the people were scattering. "So I forced myself and offered the burnt offering."[388]

Because of this misstep and another (see chapter eighty), Saul's descendants would not inherit his kingdom. It would instead pass to "a man after [God's] own heart."[389]

Questions to ponder or discuss: How was King Saul's response when confronted with his sin similar to that of Adam and Eve when God confronted them after they had eaten the forbidden fruit? Do you think God was too harsh with Saul? Why or why not?

How did you react the last time you were confronted about something you had done wrong? How *should* we react?

---

386. Some of the people hid themselves (1 Samuel 13:6), while others fled across the Jordan River (1 Samuel 13:7).

387. See for example Leviticus 1:3-17.

388. 1 Samuel 13:12

389. 1 Samuel 13:14

Chapter 79
Saul Victorious
(1 Samuel 13:15 – 14:48)

As the Philistines approached, Saul and the Israelites faced certain defeat. The Philistines not only had a larger army, but superior iron weapons instead of bronze.[390] The Philistines had barred blacksmiths from working in Israel to prevent them from using their skills to manufacture iron weapons for the Israelites.

Jonathan (Saul's son) and his armor bearer slipped out of the Israelite camp secretly and ambushed a nearby Philistine garrison, killing twenty of the enemy. This, along with a tremendous earthquake, caused panic and confusion in the ranks of the Philistine army, and they began fighting each other. Saul's army immediately attacked and the Philistines found themselves assaulted on all sides—not only by the Israelite army, but also by Israelites who had joined the Philistines but now switched sides, as well as by Israelites who had hidden themselves but now came out to fight. As a result, Saul achieved a great victory and drove the Philistines out of Israel.

Meanwhile, King Saul had given orders that no one was to eat until after the battle—perhaps to ensure that his troops would not lose their edge. But Jonathan had not heard the order, since he had slipped out of the camp prior to the Israelite attack. So when he found some honey, he ate. He later learned of the king's order and criticized it, demonstrating the independence that would characterize his future behavior.

---

390. 1 Samuel 13:22 means that Saul and Jonathan had iron weapons, unlike the other Israelites who only possessed bronze weaponry.

With the battle won, the weary and famished Israelites fell upon the animals left behind by the Philistines, killing and eating them without draining off the blood—a clear violation of the Law, which prohibited consuming blood. Saul stopped this sinful practice, but punished no one.

He was less forgiving toward his own son, for when he learned that Jonathan had consumed honey in violation of the king's order, Saul ordered his execution. Fortunately, the people refused to let Saul execute the man whose bravery and aggressiveness had been so instrumental in their victory. Jonathan was spared.

King Saul went on to defeat all of the surrounding peoples, including the Philistines,[391] Ammonites, Moabites, Edomites, and Amalekites, and the kings of Zobah (part of modern-day Syria).

Questions to ponder or discuss: Saul was tolerant of the Israelites' violation of God's law (consuming blood), but was strict toward his own son for violating the King's order (to not eat during the battle). What does this tell us about Saul and his priorities?

What is the difference between sin and crime? Which do you think is worse? Explain. What does the New Testament say about this? (See Mark 7:6-13 and Acts 5:29.[392])

---

391. The war with the Philistines continued throughout Saul's reign, per 1 Samuel 14:52.

392. In Mark 7:6-13, Jesus criticizes the Pharisees for insisting on obedience to their traditions rather than God's commands. In Acts 5:29, Peter and Jesus' other apostles respond to the high priest's command that they stop teaching about Jesus by saying, "We must obey God rather than men."

Chapter 80
King Saul's Second Big Blunder
(1 Samuel 14:49 – 15:35)

When Moses led the Israelites out of Egypt, the Amalekites carried out a cowardly attack at Rephidim against the Israelite stragglers—primarily women, children, and the old and infirm (chapter twenty-three). In addition, the Amalekites consistently allied themselves with the Israelites' enemies. So God decided to use King Saul to end this threat.[393]

He sent Samuel to Saul with instructions to attack the Amalekites and "utterly destroy all that [they have]"[394]—not merely warriors, but women, children, and animals.

Saul gathered his army and defeated the Amalekites.[395] But contrary to the Lord's instructions, Saul spared their king and the best of their animals. Then he went to Carmel where he "set up a monument for himself,"[396] and continued on to Gilgal.

Saul's disobedience led the Lord to "regret that I have made Saul king, for he has turned back from following Me and has not carried out My commands."[397] Samuel, distressed at this pronouncement, hurried to find Saul. When

---

393. This would also be a partial fulfillment of Balaam's prophecy about Amalek in Numbers 24:20.

394. 1 Samuel 15:3

395. The Lord's instructions may have been directed only at a particular branch of the Amalekites, for we will see them again when they cause trouble for David (see chapter nine-one). Alternatively, Saul must not have destroyed all of the Amalekites.

396. 1 Samuel 15:12. This is not idolatry, since the monument did not depict a god, nor did Saul seek to be worshiped. Nevertheless, it probably demonstrates Saul's arrogance, conceit, and perhaps narcissism.

397. 1 Samuel 15:10-11 (see also 1 Samuel 15:35)

they met at Gilgal, the following amusing exchange occurred:

Saul: "Blessed are you of the LORD! I have carried out the command of the LORD."[398]

Samuel: "What then is this bleating of the sheep in my ears, and the lowing of the oxen which I hear?"[399]

As before when confronted with his wrongdoing, Saul made excuses and blamed others: "They have brought them from the Amalekites, for the people spared the best of the sheep and oxen, to sacrifice to the LORD your God; but the rest we have utterly destroyed."[400] Saul blamed the people, ignoring the fact that the people would not have acted so if he as king had commanded otherwise. And he offered the excuse of good intentions—they spared the animals in order to sacrifice them to the Lord.

Samuel didn't buy it, but he seemingly offered Saul a second chance to admit his sin: "Why did you not obey the voice of the LORD, but rushed upon the spoil and did what was evil in the sight of the LORD?"[401] Unfortunately, Saul again missed his opportunity for repentance: "I did obey the voice of the LORD . . . but the people took *some* of the spoil . . . to sacrifice to the LORD your God at Gilgal."[402]

Samuel's reply pointed out what should have been obvious: "to obey is better than sacrifice."[403]

Even then, Saul offered only half-hearted repentance: "I have sinned . . . because I feared the people and listened to

---

398. 1 Samuel 15:13

399. 1 Samuel 15:14

400. 1 Samuel 15:15

401. 1 Samuel 15:19

402. 1 Samuel 15:20-21

403. 1 Samuel 15:22

their voice."[404] As a result of his disobedience on this occasion and when he offered the burnt offering instead of waiting for Samuel, Saul would soon forfeit the kingdom to David.[405]

Samuel completed what Saul had failed to, by executing Agag, king of the Amalekites.

Questions to ponder or discuss: Saul blamed the people for his own disobedience, much like Aaron did when Moses confronted him about the golden calf in Exodus 32:21-24.[406] Why is accepting responsibility for our mistakes and wrongdoing often so difficult? What are some excuses you have used to try to escape or deflect blame for your errors or misconduct? Were you successful? How do you feel about those excuses now?

---

404. 1 Samuel 15:24

405. 1 Samuel 15:23, 15:26, 15:28, and 28:18 indicate that Saul's failure to carry out the Lord's instructions regarding the Amalekites cost his descendants the throne. But see 1 Samuel 13:14, which says the Lord made this decision as a result of Saul's disobedience at Gilgal. I believe both were factors.

406. Exodus 32:21-24:

Then Moses said to Aaron, "What did this people do to you, that you have brought *such* great sin upon them?" Aaron said, "Do not let the anger of my lord burn; you know the people yourself, that they are prone to evil. For they said to me, 'Make a god for us who will go before us; for this Moses, the man who brought us up from the land of Egypt, we do not know what has become of him.' I said to them, 'Whoever has any gold, let them tear it off.' So they gave it to me, and I threw it into the fire, and out came this calf."

Chapter 81
Samuel Anoints David[407]
(1 Samuel chapter 16)

Having rejected Saul as king of Israel, the Lord sent Samuel to Bethlehem to anoint one of Jesse's sons as king.

Samuel feared King Saul's wrath if he were to learn of this mission. So the Lord devised a ruse to deceive Saul, telling Samuel to state that the purpose of his trip was merely to present a sacrifice to the Lord.

Upon arrival in Bethlehem, Jesse brought his oldest son, Eliab, to Samuel, who reasoned that this tall, sturdy young man would make an excellent king. But the Lord told Samuel that Eliab was not the one, explaining that "God *sees* not as man sees, for man looks at the outward appearance, but the LORD looks at the heart."[408]

The same thing happened with Abinadab, Shammah, and four more of Jesse's sons, for the Lord had not chosen any of them to replace Saul. That left only one—David, the youngest, who was watching his family's sheep. Samuel sent for the boy, and when he came the Lord told Samuel to anoint David as Israel's future king. David would not actually ascend the throne until after Saul's death. But from the moment of the anointing by Samuel, God's Spirit rested on David.

Meanwhile, God's Spirit left King Saul, and an evil spirit came in its place. His advisers suggested that they find

---

407. "David" may have been a title, rather than a proper name, since it appears to derive from the military title, "Davidum," which means "commander" or "general." Thus, it might have been used like the Roman title, "Caesar."

408. 1 Samuel 16:7

a musician who could sooth the king with pleasant music. The musician turned out to be David, who was probably skilled with the eight-string lyre.[409] His musical ability had the desired effect. When David played, the evil spirit fled and King Saul found some temporary peace.

David eventually became a favorite of the king, who sent a message to Jesse telling him to let David stay at court. Sometime after that, Saul made David his attendant and armor bearer.

We should note that David probably came to the king's court sometime *after* his victory over Goliath (chapter eighty-two), which occurs in 1 Samuel 17. At the time of that victory, David was still performing the duties of a shepherd for his family's sheep,[410] and Saul did not yet know his name.[411]

Questions to ponder or discuss: As noted above, 1 Samuel 16:7 says, "the LORD looks at the heart." What does the Lord see when he looks at your heart? Do you think he likes what he sees? Why or why not?

---

409. 1 Samuel 16:18-19. See the prefaces to Psalms 6 and 12, both of which provide a note "For the choir director . . . upon an eight-string lyre."

410. 1 Samuel 17:15

411. See 1 Samuel 17:55-58.

Chapter 82
David and Goliath
(1 Samuel chapter 17)

The Philistines returned to wage war against the Israelites at Socoh in the territory of Judah west of Bethlehem. Each side dug in on a hillside across a valley from each other.

They remained in this stalemate for at least forty days, and every day a Philistine named Goliath challenged the Israelites to choose a champion to fight him. But no one was brave enough to face him, for Goliath was a giant of a man. He stood over nine feet tall, wore heavy armor, and carried a thick iron-tipped spear.[412]

Jesse's three oldest sons—Eliab, Abinadab, and Shammah—were part of the Israelite army. David was still tending his family's sheep, but shuttled back and forth to the battlefield to bring food to his brothers and take news back to their father.

When David heard Goliath's challenge, he asked some of the soldiers what the king would do for the one who killed the Philistine, adding, "For who is this uncircumcised Philistine, that he should taunt the armies of the Living God?"[413] The soldiers replied that the king would make that man wealthy, give him the king's daughter in marriage, and exempt his family from taxes.

When Saul heard about David's inquiries, the king sent for the young man, who confidently announced, "your

---

412. 1 Samuel 17:4-7. Goliath's stated height may be hyperbole, since I doubt that any of the Israelites had an opportunity to actually measure him before he was slain by David.

413. 1 Samuel 17:26

servant will go and fight with this Philistine."[414] Saul was understandably hesitant to permit this since David was still only a youth. But David overcame the king's reluctance by assuring him that the young shepherd had killed lions and bears while protecting his family's sheep.

Saul offered his own armor and helmet to David, which he declined because "I have not tested *them*."[415] Since David had not worn armor before, this may mean that he believed it would constrict his movements. He instead went out to face Goliath with only a stick, a sling, and five smooth stones.

Goliath taunted and threatened David, but he confidently responded, "You come to me with a sword, a spear, and a javelin, but I come to you in the name of the LORD of hosts. . . . This day the LORD will deliver you up into my hands, and I will strike you down and remove your head from you."[416]

And that is what happened. As Goliath approached, David used his sling to cast a stone at the giant, striking him in the forehead and knocking him unconscious. David then used Goliath's own sword to kill him and cut off his head.

Seeing their champion dead, the Philistines panicked and fled, with the Israelites in pursuit as far as the border of Philistine territory.

Questions to ponder or discuss: David's tremendous faith in God is one of the attributes that made him a man after God's own heart.[417] What challenges or difficulties have

---

414. 1 Samuel 17:32

415. 1 Samuel 17:39

416. 1 Samuel 17:45-46

417. 1 Samuel 13:14

you faced in your lifetime? How did your faith in God help you face them?

Chapter 83
Saul's Jealousy
(1 Samuel 18:5 – 18:30 and 19:8 – 19:24)

Because of Saul's two big blunders, which we discussed in chapters seventy-eight and eighty, the Lord abandoned him.

Meanwhile, the Lord was with David, and he prospered in all that he did. His victory over Goliath had spread his fame throughout Israel, and he was hailed as a greater warrior than even Saul, despite the king's many victories.

King Saul made David a commander in the army, secretly hoping he would die in battle against the Philistines, but he proved more than equal to the challenge. The people adored him.

As a result, Saul became jealous and fearful. In a fit of temper, he even tried to kill David by throwing a spear at him—twice—but he escaped both times.

When Saul's daughter, Michal, fell in love with David,[418] the king offered him her hand in marriage if he would kill a hundred Philistines, "to take vengeance on the king's enemies."[419]

David killed two-hundred.

Thus, Michal became his wife. Sometime thereafter, she saved his life by helping him escape a murder plot by the king and his agents.

David fled to Samuel in Ramah, and was protected by the Lord there. Saul repeatedly sent agents to apprehend the future king, but instead of arresting him they prophesied—presumably overwhelmed by the Spirit of the Lord. In the

---

418. 1 Samuel 18:20 and 18:28

419. 1 Samuel 18:25

end, Saul went to Ramah himself and prophesied, too—but in the ultimate humiliation of this arrogant and self-centered man, he did so while naked.

Thus, Saul's efforts to have David killed were continually thwarted. But they would nevertheless continue, for Saul knew that his son Jonathan could not inherit the throne so long as David lived.[420]

Questions to ponder or discuss: 1 Samuel 18:10 and 19:9 both say that "an evil spirit" from God was upon Saul. What do you think this might mean?

According to 1 Samuel 18:7-8, Saul grew angry because women were hailing David as the greater warrior— and this happened the day *before* the "evil spirit" came upon him. 1 Samuel 18:9 adds that "Saul looked at David with suspicion from that day on." What impact do you think Saul's attitude had on God allowing this "evil spirit" to come upon him? How does jealousy damage a person's character and destroy a person's relationships with others?

---

420. 1 Samuel 20:31

Chapter 84
David and Jonathan
(1 Samuel 18:1 – 18:4, 19:1 – 19:7, and chapter 20)

Jonathan was King Saul's son and the heir to the throne—and David's best friend. 1 Samuel 18:1 and 18:4 say that Jonathan loved David as himself. They made a covenant together, and Jonathan gave his robe, armor, sword, bow, and belt to his friend.

When Saul ordered his son to have David killed, Jonathan secretly warned his friend about the order—then talked his father out of it, at least temporarily.

When David left Ramah, he came to Jonathan for help. Jonathan refused to believe that his father still wanted David dead, but nevertheless agreed to a plan David had devised. He was scheduled to eat with King Saul the next day, but planned to miss the appointment. David asked Jonathan to say that he had given his friend permission to go to Bethlehem in order to make "the yearly sacrifice there for the whole family."[421] If Saul was pleased with this news, David would know that the king was no longer angry with him. But if the king became upset at David's absence for such a worthy purpose, then Saul's evil intentions would be evident.

David and Jonathan then arranged a signal to allow them to secretly communicate about Saul's feelings toward David. In three days' time, Jonathan would shoot three arrows into a field where his friend would be hiding. If the king's anger had subsided, Jonathan would shoot the arrows to one side. Otherwise he would shoot the arrows into the distance, warning his friend to flee.

---

421. 1 Samuel 20:6

Chapter 84 – David and Jonathan

Before they parted company, Jonathan exacted a promise from his friend to be kind to Jonathan and his house forever. He would not derive any benefit from this promise personally, but it would one day help his son, Mephibosheth.

When Jonathan told his father that David had gone to Bethlehem, Saul exploded. He insisted that David must die, and accused his son of treachery by siding with his friend over his own father. Jonathan tried to argue that David had not done anything worthy of death, but the only response he received was a spear thrown at him by the king.

On the appointed day, Jonathan went into the field and used his arrows to warn David that he must flee. Soon thereafter, when they were alone in the field, Jonathan and David said goodbye and parted ways.

Questions to ponder or discuss: Jonathan, as the son of the king, had access to wealth that enabled him to give valuable gifts to David. Why does love prompt us to give to those we care about? How do you give to God? Are your gifts always reflective of your love for him?

Chapter 85
David On the Run
(1 Samuel chapters 21 – 22)

When he left Jonathan, David first fled to Nob, a city not far from Jerusalem. There he sought food and weapons, saying he was on a secret mission for the king. Ahimelech the priest had just replaced the showbread in the Tabernacle, so he gave David the old bread because it was all that was available.[422] Then the priest gave David something he probably valued much more than food—the sword of Goliath the Philistine.

After David had left, King Saul learned what Ahimelech had done. In a fit of rage, the king ordered that Ahimelech and eighty-five of his fellow priests be slain, and that the city of Nob be destroyed. Only Ahimelech's son, Abiathar, escaped to tell David what had happened.

David next went to Gath, one of the five major Philistine cities, which was ruled by the Philistine king, Achish. Unfortunately, David's reputation had preceded him. So when the king's servants thought they recognized him, he pretended to be insane—scribbling on doors and letting saliva run down his beard. When he was brought before the king, Achish sent him away, quipping, "Do I lack madmen, that you have brought this one to act the madman in my presence?"[423]

From Gath, David moved on to the cave of Adullam, which was in the "lowland"[424]—probably referring to land

---

422. 1 Samuel 21:4-6. Jesus refers to this incident in Matthew 12:3-4, Mark 2:25-26, and Luke 6:3-4.

423. 1 Samuel 21:15

424. See Joshua 15:33-35.

near the Dead Sea, which is below sea level. Here he gathered a small army of about 400 men from the poor and oppressed people who sought him out. He also sent his parents to live in Moab—a prudent precaution in view of Saul's massacre of the priests of Nob.

David subsequently moved to the forest of Hereth, having been warned by the prophet Gad to leave and go to the territory of Judah. Gad would later become David's seer,[425] and would write a history of his reign.[426]

Questions to ponder or discuss: David lied to Ahimelech in order to receive his help. When Abiathar informed David about the slaughter at Nob, the future king responded, "I have brought about *the death* of every person in your father's household."[427] To what degree do you think David bore any moral responsibility for what happened to the priests and people of Nob?

Suppose that David knew that he would receive no help in Nob if he told the truth. Would that justify his lie? Why or why not? Under what circumstances would you be willing to lie?

---

425. 2 Samuel 24:11 and 2 Chronicles 29:25

426. See 1 Chronicles 29:29.

427. 1 Samuel 22:22

Chapter 86
David's Narrow Escapes
(1 Samuel chapters 23 – 24)

David's small army grew to about 600 men. The Lord sent him and his small force to deliver the town of Keilah from the Philistines who were plundering it. When King Saul learned of this, he summoned an army to attack David at Keilah. David, having been warned by God that the men of Keilah would deliver him to Saul, escaped with his men to Horesh in the wilderness of Ziph. This was in the territory of the tribe of Judah, west of the Dead Sea.

At Horesh, Jonathan came to encourage David and to make a covenant with him. But David had to flee again when the Ziphites betrayed him by sending word of his presence to Saul.

David traveled south to the wilderness of Maon. Saul pursued him there and at one point the two were on opposite sides of the same mountain. As Saul closed in, word came to him that the Philistines were attacking, leading him to abandon the pursuit and return to battle the Philistines. David and his men moved east to Engedi, an oasis near the western shore of the Dead Sea.

Saul defeated the Philistines, then resumed his pursuit of David with an army of 3,000 men. Upon reaching Engedi, Saul went into a cave to relieve himself, no doubt seeking a bit of privacy. Ironically, he entered the cave where David and his men were hiding. His men urged him to take advantage of this opportunity to kill the king, but David refused. Instead, he merely cut off a piece of Saul's robe (which the king may have removed when he entered the cave). After Saul left, David called out to him, and produced the piece of robe as evidence of David's loyalty and respect for the king.

Chapter 86 – David's Narrow Escapes

Shamed by David's actions, Saul abandoned his pursuit and returned home after exacting a promise from David not to harm Saul's descendants.

Questions to ponder or discuss: Think about a time when someone—perhaps a parent, spouse, or friend—has forgiven you for hurting them. How did that make you feel? Is it harder to forgive someone you dislike than it is to forgive a friend? Why or why not? Do you think David's actions toward Saul reflect what Jesus meant when he told us to love our enemies?[428] Explain.

---

428. See, for example, Matthew 5:44: "But I say to you, love your enemies and pray for those who persecute you. . . ." See also, Luke 6:27.

Chapter 87
David and Abigail
(1 Samuel 25:1 – 25:43)

Samuel died and was buried in Ramah, after which David and his men went to the wilderness of Paran[429]—also known as the wilderness of Zin[430]—a desert area southwest of the Dead Sea, between the Sinai Peninsula and Palestine. Kadesh-barnea was located there. The Israelites had resided in the wilderness of Paran after leaving Mount Sinai, and waited there when they sent the spies into Canaan.[431]

David sent some of his men to ask for food from a wealthy man named Nabal, whose sheep and shepherds David's men had been protecting. Nabal gave the men only insults. So David prepared to descend upon this ungrateful fellow with 400 men, intending to kill him.

Nabal's servants told his wife, Abigail, what had happened, and she rushed to avoid disaster. She prepared a large offering of food to placate David and his men, then went out to meet them on their way. Falling at his feet, she implored him to accept her food offering and forgive both her and her foolish husband, lest David become guilty of killing without adequate cause. Impressed by both her gift and her humility, David accepted the food and left with his men.

After Abigail told Nabal how close to death he had come, "his heart died within him"[432]—presumably he had a

---

429. Ishmael, the half-brother of Isaac, lived in Paran. (Genesis 21:21) Ishmael was Abraham's son by Sarah's Egyptian maid, Hagar. See Genesis 16:1-15.

430. Compare Numbers 13:26 and Numbers 20:1

431. See Numbers 10:11-12, 12:16, 13:25-26.

432. 1 Samuel 25:37

heart attack. He died ten days later. When David learned what had happened, he took Abigail as his wife. He also married Ahinoam of Jezreel.

Questions to ponder or discuss: In light of Nabal's callous refusal of hospitality—which he could easily afford—to men who had safeguarded his property, would his murder have been justifiable? Can two wrongs ever make a right? Why or why not?

Chapter 88
David's Mercy Toward Saul
(1 Samuel chapter 26)

When David and his men returned to the wilderness of Ziph, the Ziphites again betrayed him by disclosing his location to King Saul at Gibeah. The king immediately led 3,000 men to the hill of Hachilah, where the Ziphites had said he would find David.

David's spies informed him Saul was coming, as well as where he was. So David and his nephew Abishai[433] snuck into the king's camp undetected, "because a sound sleep from the LORD had fallen on them."[434] Resisting Abishai's advice to kill, David stole Saul's spear and water jug, in order to demonstrate how close the king had come to assassination if David had wanted to do so.

He then went to a nearby mountain top, some distance from the king's encampment, and called out to the captain of Saul's army, Abner,[435] pointing out that he had failed in his duty to protect the king—and holding up the king's spear and water jug as proof.

As before at the cave at Engedi, King Saul realized he had been at David's mercy, yet had survived. Humbled once again, the king withdrew his army.

Questions to ponder or discuss: In 1 Samuel 26:21, Saul confesses, "I have sinned." This may indicate that he felt guilty

---

433. Abishai (aka Abshai) was the son of David's sister, Zeruiah. See 1 Samuel 26:6 and 1 Chronicles 2:13-16. Abishai was one of David's "mighty men," his best and most devoted soldiers. See 1 Chronicles 11:10-12:15.

434. 1 Samuel 26:6-12 (the quotation is from 1 Samuel 26:12)

435. Abner was Saul's uncle. See 1 Samuel 14:50.

about his unjust treatment of David. But an alternative explanation is that David's public demonstration of Saul's unfairness—in the presence of the king's entire army—left him little choice but to back down. Which explanation do you think is more consistent with Saul's character? Explain. Why do people sometimes do the right thing only when they feel pressured by the scrutiny of others?

Chapter 89
David Among the Philistines
(1 Samuel 27:1 – 28:2 and 29:1 – 30:5; 1 Chronicles 12:1 – 22)

Fearing that Saul would continue to pursue him, David led his men back to the one place he knew Saul would not follow—the territory of the Philistines.[436] This time Achish, king of Gath, welcomed David and his men, probably because he was now believed to be Saul's enemy (the enemy of my enemy is my friend). David stayed among the Philistines for sixteen months.[437]

Achish allowed David to live in the city of Ziklag,[438] which had once belonged to the tribes of Judah and Simeon and was probably near the border.[439] Since David was from the tribe of Judah,[440] Ziklag may have been friendly and familiar territory for him. Here David began to gather an impressive army, adding to his ranks "mighty men"[441] from the

---

436. 1 Samuel 27:1-4

437. 1 Samuel 27:7

438. 1 Samuel 27:5-6. Ziklag was located south of Gath and east of Gaza, in southern Palestine.

439. See Joshua 15:31 and 19:5. The territory allotted to the tribe of Simeon was "in the midst of the inheritance of the sons of Judah." (Joshua 19:1) So it seems that the two tribes shared the same territory.

440. See 1 Chronicles 2:1-15.

441. The thirty-seven "mighty men" are listed in 2 Samuel 23:8-39. See also 2 Chronicles 11:26-47. These were men who fought at David's side when he defeated his enemies and built his kingdom. Uriah the Hittite, the husband of Bathsheba, was one of these mighty men, per 2 Samuel 23:39 and 1 Chronicles 11:44.

tribes of Gad, Judah, Manasseh, and Saul's own tribe, Benjamin.[442]

The Philistine king believed that David had become repugnant to his fellow Israelites—a misconception David was careful to promote. When he and his men raided the neighboring Geshurites,[443] Girzites, and Amalekites, he lied to Achish, telling him that the raids had been conducted against Israelite territory.[444]

Near the end of David's sixteen months with the Philistines, they mobilized their armies in Aphek[445] to go to war against Saul. David went with King Achish as his bodyguard.[446] This could have placed David in a difficult position—he would have to either fight against his fellow Israelites or betray his Philistine benefactor. Fortunately, the other Philistine commanders insisted that David and his men be sent back, arguing that the quickest way for David to reconcile with Saul would be to help him defeat the Philistines.[447]

---

442. 1 Chronicles 12:1-22

443. The land of the Geshurites was one of several areas where the Israelites failed to take possession of land given to them by the Lord. See Joshua 13:2 and 13:15.

444. 1 Samuel 27:8-12.

445. 1 Samuel 29:1. Per Joshua 19:30, Aphek was within the territory of the tribe of Asher, whose lands bordered the Mediterranean Sea west and northwest of the Sea of Galilee. Aphek was where the Philistines camped prior to the Battle of Ebenezer. (1 Samuel 4:1)

446. 1 Samuel 28:1-2 and 29:1-2

447. 1 Samuel 29:3-9 and 1 Chronicles 12:19

David and his men returned to Ziklag,[448] where they discovered that the Amalekites had raided and burned the city, and abducted all of the women and children.[449]

Questions to ponder or discuss: David pretended to be an enemy of the Israelites in order to receive favorable treatment from the Philistines. This was at least the second time David had lied to gain an advantage. Do you consider this lie to be harmless? Why or why not? Can some lies be good? Explain. Under what circumstances should we feel obligated to tell the truth?

---

448. Ziklag was about seventy miles south of Aphek.

449. 1 Samuel 29:10 – 30:3

Chapter 90
Saul and the Witch of En-dor
(1 Samuel 28:3 – 28:25)

As we saw in the last chapter, the Philistines prepared to go to war against Saul and the Israelites. The Bible doesn't tell us what prompted this new war, but it was preceded by Saul's order to remove all mediums and spiritists from Israel. Perhaps the Philistines interpreted this as an act of rebellion rather than merely a religious revival, since in those days (and throughout most of history) rulers viewed religious and civic loyalty as inseparable.

The Philistines marched east from Aphek through the Valley of Jezreel[450] in central Israel to Shunem.[451] Saul gathered his forces in Jezreel, across the valley south of Shunem, then retreated to Mount Gilboa[452] in search of high ground before the approaching battle.

The might of the Philistine army so frightened Saul that he sought a word from the Lord—but the Lord had forsaken him and was silent. So Saul instructed his servants to find a medium who could contact the ghost of Samuel. Such action not only violated God's law, which prohibited the use of mediums and spiritists,[453] but also Saul's own order.

Nevertheless, Saul's servants told him about a female medium—what we might call a witch—in En-dor. Saul went

---

450. The Valley of Jezreel is where Gideon's victory over the Midianites occurred.

451. Shunem was within the territory of the tribe of Issachar. See Joshua 19:17-18. Issachar's territory was in central Israel, southwest of the Sea of Galilee.

452. 1 Samuel 28:4 and 31:1. Mount Gilboa is about twenty miles southwest of the Sea of Galilee, and about ten miles west of the Jordan River.

453. See Leviticus 19:26, 19:31, 20:6, and 20:27, and Deuteronomy 18:9-14.

to the woman in disguise and convinced her to call up the spirit of Samuel. This must have been a remarkable journey, for En-dor was about seven miles north of Gilboa—on the other side of the Philistine encampment. Such was Saul's desperation.

When Samuel appeared, Saul asked what he should do. The report Samuel gave him was as bad as Saul could have imagined. Samuel said the Philistines would win the battle, and Saul and his sons would die. Terrified by this prophecy, Saul fell on his face. But after some urging by the woman, he ate and left.

Questions to ponder or discuss: I believe this is the low point of Saul's spiritual journey. Forsaken by God and desperate for guidance, he deliberately turned to evil by seeking out a medium. What have been the low points of your spiritual journey? Who or what brought you out of them?

Have you sought guidance from God and felt that you did not receive it? If so, how did you feel about that? What did you do about it? How did it turn out?

Chapter 91
David and the Amalekites
(1 Samuel 30:6 – 30:31)

When we left David in chapter eighty-nine, he had been sent home by the Philistines and arrived to find his city burned and the women and children abducted.

Facing a possible mutiny among his men because of this disaster, David consulted the Lord about what he should do. The Lord told David to pursue the Amalekites, promising that he would be victorious.

David set out with 600 men, but left 200 behind at the brook Besor because they were too exhausted to continue. Further on, David encountered an Egyptian who had been an Amalekite slave. The Amalekites had abandoned him when he became sick, and he had been without food or water for three days. David and his men fed him and promised him safety if he would lead them to the Amalekites.

Guided by the Egyptian, David and his men were able to ambush the bandits during their victory celebration. They rescued everyone who had been taken, plus sheep, cattle, and other livestock belonging to the Amalekites.

During the return trip, a dispute arose. Some of the 400 men who had battled the Amalekites refused to share the spoils with the 200 who had stayed behind. David settled this quarrel by pointing out that their victory was the Lord's doing, and that those who remained at the brook had guarded everyone's baggage. Thus, David ordered that all share equally, which became a law in Israel from that time forward.

To win friends in Judah, David sent some of the Amalekite loot to various cities there, as well as to the elders of Judah. This generosity would soon pay off for him.

The Old Testament Made Simple (Part 1)

Questions to ponder or discuss: Does David's decision regarding the victory spoils remind you of Jesus' parable of
the vineyard owner who gave all of his workers a denarius
regardless of how long they had worked in the vineyard?[454]
How are the two stories similar? How are they different?
Should a Christian who lives his entire life in a country with
freedom of religion receive the same reward from God as a
Christian who lived in a land where Christians were perse-
cuted?[455] Why or why not?

---

454. See Matthew 20:1-16.

455. This question could be expanded almost without limit. For example,
should a missionary and the people who finance his or her mission work
receive the same reward? Should a pastor and the members of his or her
flock receive the same reward?

Chapter 92
The Deaths of Saul and Jonathan
(1 Samuel chapter 31; 1 Chronicles chapter 10)

As Samuel predicted, the battle against the Philistines went badly for Saul and the Israelites. The Philistines routed Saul's army, sending them fleeing to Mount Gilboa. There Jonathan and two other sons of Saul—Abinadab and Malchishua—were slain, along with many of the Israelite soldiers. Saul was not killed, but was badly wounded by Philistine archers.[456]

Seeing that the battle was lost and that his own death was imminent, Saul ordered his armor-bearer to kill him so the Philistines would not be able to torture or make sport of him. When his armor-bearer refused, Saul committed suicide with his own sword. His armor-bearer killed himself the same way.[457]

The Philistines found the bodies the next day. They cut off Saul's head, sent his weapons to the temples of their gods, and fastened the bodies of Saul and his three sons to a wall in Beth-shan,[458] a town in central Palestine near the Jordan River, within the territory of the tribe of Manasseh.[459]

The men of Jabesh-gilead refused to permit this desecration of the body of the king who had saved them from the Ammonites. The men walked all night to Beth-shan[460] and

---

456. 1 Samuel 31:1-3

457. 1 Samuel 31:4-6

458. 1 Samuel 31:8-10

459. See Joshua 17:11. Although Beth-shan and several other areas were actually within the territorial boundaries of Asher and Issachar, they were allotted to Manasseh. See Joshua 17:12. At that time the Canaanites had not been driven from these areas, per Joshua 17:13.

460. This would have been a distance of about twelve miles.

brought the bodies back to Jabesh, where they were burned. The residents of Jabesh buried the bones and mourned Saul and his sons for seven days.[461]

As a result of Saul's defeat, the Philistines captured and occupied Israelite territory in the Valley of Jezreel, as well as east of the Jordan River.[462]

Questions to ponder or discuss: Do you believe suicide is a sin? Why or why not? Are there any circumstances under which you would consider taking your own life? Explain.

---

461. 1 Samuel 31:11-13

462. 1 Samuel 31:7 and 1 Chronicles 10:7

Chapter 93
David Becomes King of Judah
(2 Samuel chapters 1 – 2)

David was in Ziklag when an Amalekite brought news of Israel's defeat and the deaths of Saul and Jonathan. After mourning them for a time, David sought the Lord's guidance, who instructed him to go to Hebron. There the men of Judah anointed him as king of Judah.[463] David was only thirty years old.[464] He would reign as king of Judah for seven-and-a-half years, and take four more wives.[465] He also had six sons while in Hebron, [466] including Amnon and Absalom, both of whom we will see again.

Meanwhile, the rest of the Israelites recognized a different king—Ish-bosheth, a son of Saul. After Saul's death, Abner, the commander of Saul's army, brought Ish-bosheth to Mahanaim, where he was anointed as king of Israel. Ish-bosheth, which means "man of shame," was forty years old

---

463. 2 Samuel 2:1-4 and 1 Chronicles 11:1-3. Among David's supporters were men from each of the other tribes. They wanted to make him king over all of Israel. See 1 Chronicles 12:1-37.

464. 2 Samuel 5:4

465. David's four new wives were: (1) Maacah, daughter of Talmai, king of Geshur; (2) Haggith; (3) Abital; and (4) Eglah. See 2 Samuel 2:11, 3:3-5; 1 Chronicles 3:1-4. Having many wives was contrary to God's instructions for Israel's future kings. See Deuteronomy 17:17.

466. The six sons born to David in Hebron were: (1) Amnon, son of Ahinoam, (2) Chileab aka Daniel, son of Abigail, (3) Absalom, son of Maacah, (4) Adonijah, son of Haggith, (5) Shaphatiah, son of Abital, and (6) Ithream, son of Eglah. 2 Samuel 3:2-5 and 1 Chronicles 3:1-4. He would have thirteen more sons while he was king in Jerusalem. See 1 Chronicles 3:5-9.

and would reign for only two years.[467] The real power in Israel during this time appears to have been Abner, whom Ish-bosheth feared.[468]

Having two kings sparked a war between the two kingdoms. The war may have started at Gibeon, near the border between Benjamin and Judah. There Abner challenged David's nephew and future commander, Joab, to a contest—twelve men from Benjamin against twelve men from Judah. The encounter turned deadly and sparked a battle in which Joab's soldiers routed those of Abner.

While fleeing the battlefield, Abner was pursued by another of David's nephews, Asahel, the brother of Abishai and Joab.[469] When Asahel would not relent in his pursuit, Abner stopped to face him and killed him. This would soon cost Abner his own life.

Questions to ponder or discuss: The Amalekite who brought the news of Saul's death claimed to have killed him (Saul actually killed himself), and as proof presented his crown and bracelet to David. The Amalekite thought this lie would curry favor with David,[470] who instead ordered the man's execution for the offense of regicide (that is, murdering a king). How do you feel about what David did? Should

467. 2 Samuel 2:10. The Bible does not explain the discrepancy between the length of David's reign as king of Judah—seven and one-half years—and Ish-bosheth's shorter two-year reign as king of Israel. Perhaps Ish-bosheth's reign did not commence until after David had been king for awhile, thus inciting a war over succession to the throne. Or perhaps others reigned in Israel after Ish-bosheth's death and before David became king over Israel. Or perhaps it was a combination of both.

468. 2 Samuel 3:11; see also 2 Samuel 3:6

469. Asahel, Abishai, and Joab were all children of David's sister, Zeruiah. See 2 Samuel 2:18, 1 Samuel 26:6, and 1 Chronicles 2:13-16.

470. See 2 Samuel 4:9-10.

David have left the Amalekite's fate in God's hands? Why or why not?

A bias is "a preference or inclination that inhibits impartial judgment."[471] We all have biases. For example, we may be biased in favor of friends and family members, or our favorite sports teams, or our political party. David had a bias against regicide, since he was a king himself. When is it all right to let our biases impact our decision making? When is it not all right?

---

471. The quote is from *The American Heritage Dictionary of the English Language*, edited by William Morris (American Heritage Publishing Co., New York, 1975).

Chapter 94
David Becomes King of Israel
(2 Samuel 3:1 – 5:5)

Judah was already winning the war with Israel when Abner, Israel's military commander, offered to switch sides. The reason for Abner's betrayal of his king is unclear. He may have been motivated by Ish-bosheth's accusation that Abner had slept with one of King Saul's concubines—an accusation which Abner clearly resented. But perhaps he simply saw that David was winning the war and wanted to be on the side of the eventual victor. In any event, David welcomed Abner's cooperation, with one stipulation—that he return David's wife, Michal, whom Saul had married to another man after David fled.[472]

When Abner came to Hebron, David welcomed him with a feast. Abner promised to deliver Israel into David's hands, then left in peace. But Joab secretly summoned Abner back—and murdered him. Joab suspected Abner of duplicity,[473] but Joab's true motive was revenge for Abner's killing of Asahel, the brother of Joab and Abishai.[474]

Abner's death was a crippling blow for Ish-bosheth, who seems to have been a coward at heart.[475] Before long

---

472. 1 Samuel 25:44 and 2 Samuel 3:15. Ish-bosheth was actually the one who sent Michal back to David, perhaps in an effort to make peace between the two kingdoms. See 2 Samuel 3:14-16.

473. This does not appear to have been the case. See 2 Samuel 3:9-10 and 3:17-19.

474. 2 Samuel 3:23-27. David did not approve of Joab's actions. See 2 Samuel 3:28-37. Nevertheless, David left it to the Lord and to Solomon to punish Joab (2 Samuel 3:29 and 3:39, and 1 Kings 2:5-6)—perhaps because Joab was his nephew.

475. See 2 Samuel 3:11 and 4:1.

two of his army commanders assassinated him.[476] They brought the deposed king's head to David, expecting that they would be favorably received. Instead, as he did with the dishonest Amalekite, David ordered their execution.

Sometime after this, the elders of Israel offered David the throne of Israel, making David king of both Judah and Israel. He would rule them for thirty-three more years.

Questions to ponder or discuss: As noted above, Abner may have double-crossed Ish-bosheth in order to be on the winning side. What are you willing to do to win? What are you *not* willing to do to win? Would your answers change depending on what you were trying to win (for example, a game or a war)?

---

476. The names of the murderers were Baanah and Rechab.

Chapter 95
King David's Power Grows
(2 Samuel 5:6 – 5:25; 1 Chronicles 11:4 – 11:17 and 14:1 – 14:7)

David laid siege to the city of Jerusalem (also known as Jebus), a stronghold occupied by the Jebusites.[477] They believed they were safe inside the city walls, but David's men were able to sneak in and capture the city by going through the "water tunnel."[478] This was a shaft leading from the city to the Spring Gihon, which supplied the city's water.[479] David made Joab his chief commander after this battle because he courageously led the fight and was the first Israelite to kill a Jebusite.[480]

The city became David's permanent residence, earning it the title "the city of David."[481] There he built his house, using materials and craftsmen supplied by Hiram, king of Tyre.[482] He also took more wives and concubines, and had many additional children.[483] 2 Samuel 5:10 tells us that "David became greater and greater, for the LORD God of hosts was with him."

David's growing strength caused the Philistines to view him as a rival rather than a vassal or an ally. So they

---

477. 2 Samuel 5:6 and 1 Chronicles 11:4

478. 2 Samuel 5:6-8.

479. This shaft was found in 1867 by British Army Captain Charles Warren, and is now known as "Warren's Shaft."

480. 1 Chronicles 11:6

481. 2 Samuel 5:9 and 1 Chronicles 11:7. Bethlehem is also known as the "city of David" because his family was from there. See Luke 2:4, 2:11.

482. 2 Samuel 5:11-12 and 1 Chronicles 14:1

483. 2 Samuel 5:13-16 and 1 Chronicles 14:3-7

brought their army to the Valley of Rephaim, southwest of Jerusalem, to crush him.[484] David asked the Lord if he should fight the Philistines, and the Lord promised him victory.[485] Sure enough, David defeated them at Baal-perazim.[486]

Sometime later the Philistines came against David again, probably with a larger force, and camped again in the Valley of Rephaim and at Bethlehem.[487] David retreated to the cave of Adullam near the Dead Sea and sought the advice of the Lord.[488] This time he told David to "circle around behind them"[489]—presumably a surprise attack from a direction the Philistines would not expect. This strategy worked and David drove the Philistines out of Israel as far as Gezer.[490]

Questions to ponder or discuss: On two different occasions, David sought the Lord's counsel before he acted. What decisions have you sought the Lord's counsel about in the past? How did you seek to discern God's will for those decisions? What decisions will you seek the Lord's counsel about in the future?

---

484. 2 Samuel 5:17-18 and 1 Chronicles 14:8-9

485. 2 Samuel 5:19 and 1 Chronicles 14:10

486. 2 Samuel 5:20 and 1 Chronicles 14:11

487. 2 Samuel 5:22 and 23:13-14, and 1 Chronicles 11:15-16

488. 2 Samuel 5:23 and 23:13, and 1 Chronicles 11:15 and 14:14

489. 2 Samuel 5:23 and 1 Chronicles 14:14

490. 2 Samuel 5:25 and 1 Chronicles 14:16-17. Gezer was a strategic city located almost twenty miles west-northwest of Jerusalem, along a principal road from Jerusalem to the Mediterranean coast. Gezer was in the southern portion of the territory of Ephraim, in central Israel. See Joshua 21:21. David's victory pushed the Philistines out of the Palestinian hill country, and back onto the plains closer to the Mediterranean Sea.

Chapter 96
King David and the Ark
(2 Samuel 6:1 – 6:19; 1 Chronicles chapter 13 and 15:1 – 16:3)

When we last saw the Ark of the Covenant, it was resting in Kiriath-jearim (also known as Baalah or Baale-judah[491]) where it had remained for twenty years. King David led the Israelites there with the intention of bringing the Ark to Jerusalem.

They placed the Ark on an ox cart, driven by Uzzah and Ahio, sons of Abinadab.[492] This was not how God had instructed the Israelites to handle the Ark. As we saw in chapter twenty-seven, the Levites were supposed to carry it, using poles inserted through rings on its sides, for no one was allowed to touch the Ark.[493] This carelessness would have tragic results.

The people proceeded with great celebration, and all seemed well—until the oxen nearly upset the cart. Uzzah reached out to steady the Ark, and the Lord struck him dead on the spot, "for his irreverence."[494]

Uzzah's death both angered and frightened King David, who immediately stopped the procession and left the Ark at the house of Obed-edom the Gittite.[495] The Ark re-

---

491. See 2 Samuel 6:2 and 1 Chronicles 13:6.

492. 2 Samuel 6:3 and 1 Chronicles 13:7. One of David's older brothers was named Abinadab, but the Bible does not tell us if this was the same Abinadab.

493. Exodus 25:12-15 and Numbers 4:15

494. 2 Samuel 6:6-7 and 1 Chronicles 13:9-10

495. 2 Samuel 6:9-10 and 1 Chronicles 13:11-13

mained with Obed-edom for three months, during which time the Lord blessed him and his entire household.[496]

Obed-edom's good fortune renewed David's determination to bring the Ark to Jerusalem. He realized that the problem did not lie with the Ark itself, but with how it had been mishandled.[497] So when he went to retrieve it from Obed-edom, he ensured that everything was done properly according to the Law. He commanded the priests Zadok and Abiathar to consecrate themselves, along with the Levites, in preparation for this holy task.[498] He ordered that "No one is to carry the ark of God but the Levites,"[499] and they were to carry the ark on their shoulders using the poles made for that purpose.[500]

This time all went well. The Ark was brought to Jerusalem with great celebration and placed in a tent David had prepared for it.[501]

Questions to ponder or discuss: Was it fair of the Lord to kill Uzzah? Why or why not? Is it fair that people sometimes suffer because of the mistakes of their leaders? Explain. Give examples—either from history or from your own life—of when you have seen people suffer as a result of their leaders' mistakes.

---

496. 2 Samuel 6:11 and 1 Chronicles 13:14

497. See 1 Chronicles 15:11-13

498. 1 Chronicles 15:12

499. 1 Chronicles 15:2

500. 1 Chronicles 15:15

501. 2 Samuel 6:17 and 1 Chronicles 15:1, 16:1. This tent was *not* the Tabernacle. 1 Chronicles 16:39 and 21:29 make clear that the Tabernacle and the bronze altar were in Gibeon at this time.

Chapter 97
David and Michal
(2 Samuel 6:14 – 23 and 1 Chronicles 15:29)

When King David brought the Ark to Jerusalem the people celebrated "with shouting and the sound of the trumpet."[502] In addition, David provided for music, with singers, harps, lyres, and loud cymbals.[503] The king joined in this joyous celebration, leaping and "dancing before the LORD with all *his* might."[504]

Michal, David's first wife, did not participate in the festivity. This daughter of Saul remained inside where she was able to observe her husband's behavior—"and she despised him in her heart."[505] She believed the king was making a fool of himself. When David finally came inside, she told him so, with words dripping in sarcasm and contempt:

> How the king of Israel distinguished himself
> today. He uncovered himself today in the eyes
> of his servants' maids as one of the foolish ones
> shamelessly uncovers himself.[506]

King David protested that this was no ordinary party, but a celebration for the Lord, who had raised David up to be king in place of Michal's own father, King Saul. In lan-

---

502. 2 Samuel 6:15. In this context, "trumpet" refers to the shofar (or shophar), the ram's horn, which was often blown as part of religious ceremonies and festivals.

503. 1 Chronicles 15:16 and 15:28

504. 2 Samuel 6:14 and 6:16

505. 2 Samuel 6:16 and 1 Chronicles 15:29

506. 2 Samuel 6:20

guage that foreshadows Matthew 23:12,[507] David pointed out that through his humility he would be distinguished in the eyes of the people.[508]

2 Samuel 6:23 notes that Michal remained childless until the day she died, implying that she and David never reconciled after this incident.

Questions to ponder or discuss: Michal's vanity would not allow her to look foolish, even for God. Have you known people like that? Have you ever been like that? Explain.

---

507. Matthew 23:12: "Whoever exalts himself shall be humbled; and whoever humbles himself shall be exalted." See also Luke 1:52, 14:11, and 18:14; James 4:10; and 1 Peter 5:6.

508. 2 Samuel 6:21-22

Chapter 98
King David Builds His Kingdom[509]
(2 Samuel chapters 8 and 10, and 21:15 – 21:22; 1 Chronicles
chapters 18 – 19, and 20:4 – 20:8)

As we saw in chapter ninety-five, David defeated the
Philistines and drove them out of the hill country of Palestine, but only as far as Gezer. The Philistines regrouped and
tried again, forcing David to defeat them repeatedly in a se-
ries of battles.

In the first of these encounters, a mighty Philistine
warrior named Ishbi-benob almost killed David before Abishai came to his rescue. After this David's men would not let
him fight in the front lines anymore,[510] although he probably
continued to plan and direct the wars.

In subsequent conflicts at Gezer[511] and Gob,[512] two of
David's "mighty men"[513] led the Israelites to victory. The de-

---

509. I have made certain assumptions about the order in which these
wars occurred, because 2 Samuel and 1 Chronicles do not appear to be in
chronological order. For example, chapter seven of 2 Samuel describes
events that occurred when "the LORD had given [David] rest on every
side from all his enemies" (2 Samuel 7:1), but subsequent chapters describe David's many wars against the surrounding nations, which presumably preceded the events of chapter seven. Similarly, 2 Samuel 8:1
and 1 Chronicles 18:1 summarize David's conquest of the Philistines,
which appears to be described in greater detail in 2 Samuel 21:15-22 and
1 Chronicles 20:4-8.

510. 2 Samuel 21:15-17

511. 1 Chronicles 20:4-5

512. 2 Samuel 21:18-19

513. Sibbecai the Hushathite and Elhanan son of Jair (or Jaare-oregim)
the Bethlehmite. See 1 Chronicles 20:4-5 and 2 Samuel 21:18-19. 1 Chronicles 11:26 says that Elhanan was one of David's mighty men, and
1 Chronicles 11:29 similarly lists Sibbecai among them.

cisive final confrontation occurred at Gath, one of the five major Philistine cities. David was again victorious and captured the city.[514]

With his border secure in the west, David next found himself at war with the Ammonites to the east. The chain of events that resulted in this war began when Nahash, the Ammonite king, died. David sent messengers to express his condolences, but Nahash's son, Hanun, treated the messengers as spies, shaving their beards and cutting off their clothing below the hips.[515] Probably realizing that this insult would not go unchallenged, Hanun prepared for war by hiring mercenaries from Aram and Zobah (both in modern-day Syria), and Tob (Jephthah's stronghold, per Judges 11:3 and 11:5).[516] David responded by mobilizing the Israelite army, under the command of Joab.[517]

The Ammonites laid a trap for Joab, and he fell into it. He found himself surrounded by the Ammonite army on one side and the Arameans on the other. So he divided his forces, placing himself in command of the Israelites facing the Arameans, and Abishai in command of those facing the Ammonites.[518] When the Arameans were beaten and fled, the Ammonites also ran away.[519]

More battles against the Arameans and Hadadezer king of Zobah followed, with David inflicting crushing de-

514. 2 Samuel 8:1 and 21:20-22; 1 Chronicles 20:6-8

515. 2 Samuel 10:1-5; 1 Chronicles 19:1-5

516. 2 Samuel 10:6; 1 Chronicles 19:6-7

517. 2 Samuel 10:7; 1 Chronicles 19:8

518. 2 Samuel 10:8-12; 1 Chronicles 19:10-13

519. 2 Samuel 10:13-14; 1 Chronicles 19:14-15

feats on them.[520] This led Hadadezer and the Arameans to make peace.[521]

With their Aramean allies sidelined, the Ammonites were quickly subdued by Joab and the Israelites.[522] David also defeated the Moabites, the Amalekites, and the Edomites.[523] He placed garrisons in many of these lands, and as was customary at that time he received tribute from them—some of which he dedicated to the Lord.[524]

Questions to ponder or discuss: We tend to honor and glorify leaders like David who are victorious in war—men like George Washington, Abraham Lincoln, Ulysses Grant, and George Patton.[525] Why do you think we give such honor and glory to our victorious leaders?

Are we glorifying war when we do this? Why or why not? *Should* we glorify war? Explain.

---

520. 2 Samuel 8:3-5, 10:15-18; 1 Chronicles 19:15-18. One of David's victories over Hadadezer occurred at Helam, per 2 Samuel 10:16-17. Helam was located near the northern border of Zobah, in what is now Syria.

521. 2 Samuel 10:19; 1 Chronicles 19:19. David's victory over Hadaezer also won him an ally in Tou (aka Toi), king of Hamath, who was an enemy of Hadaezer. See 2 Samuel 8:9-10 and 1 Chronicles 18:9-10. Hamath was located in what is now western Syria.

522. 1 Chronicles 20:1-3; see also 2 Samuel 12:26-31

523. 2 Samuel 8:2, 8:12, 8:14; 1 Chronicles 18:2, 18:11-13

524. 2 Samuel 8:6-8, 8:11-12, 8:14; 1 Chronicles 18:6-8, 18:11, 19:19

525. We sometimes do this for military leaders who were *not* victorious, although I believe it is less common. Examples include George Armstrong Custer, who died in the Battle of the Little Bighorn in Montana, and William Barrett Travis, commander at the Alamo.

Chapter 99
David and the Temple
(2 Samuel chapter 7)

When at last the king's enemies had been subdued, David felt guilty that the Ark was sitting in a tent instead of a proper building. He consulted Nathan the prophet about building a "house" for the Lord—that is, the Jewish temple. Nathan said to go ahead.

But that same night the Lord countermanded Nathan's advice, explaining to the king that since he was "a man of war" and had shed blood, his descendant would build the temple instead.[526] However, the Lord promised David that his line and kingdom would be established forever through his descendant.

The king reacted with praise and thanksgiving to God for raising David from obscurity to become king, and for redeeming the people of Israel and doing great things for them.

Questions to ponder or discuss: Sometimes God's plans for us do not coincide with our plans, requiring that our plans change. Has this happened to you? How did you react in those moments? How is David a good example for us in that regard?

---

526. 1 Chronicles 28:3

Chapter 100
Mephibosheth
(2 Samuel chapter 9)

David, remembering his love for Jonathan, made inquiries about whether any of King Saul's descendants were still alive, and learned from one of Saul's former servants, Ziba, that Jonathan had a surviving son named Mephibosheth.

This grandson of Saul was crippled because of an accident that occurred shortly after his father and grandfather were killed. Mephibosheth was only five years old at the time. News of the death of Saul and Jonathan prompted Mephibosheth's nurse to take the boy and flee. But in her haste the boy fell and was seriously injured. As a result, he was lame in both feet.[527]

David summoned Mephibosheth, who prostrated himself before the king, no doubt fearing the worst. But David surprised the young man by awarding him the land and possessions that had formerly belonged to his grandfather, Saul, and by insisting that Mephibosheth dine regularly at the king's table as if he were one of David's own sons.

David instructed Ziba that he, along with his fifteen sons and twenty servants, would serve Mephibosheth and cultivate the land for him. Jonathan's surviving son lived in Jerusalem and had a son of his own named Mica.

Question to ponder or discuss: David's generosity toward Mephibosheth is an excellent example of grace—unmerited favor—in the Old Testament. Mephibosheth had done nothing to deserve the kindness he received. Aside from God's

---

527. 2 Samuel 4:4

220

grace, what are some examples of grace that you have received from others in your own life (for example, from parents, friends, spouse, etc.)?

Chapter 101
David and Bathsheba
(2 Samuel 11:1 – 12:14)

At a time when Israel was at war with the Ammonites, David remained in Jerusalem. While walking around
on the roof of the king's palace, he saw a beautiful woman
bathing—Bathsheba (aka Bath-shua),[528] the wife of Urriah
the Hittite, one of the mighty men. The king sent for her, and
she became pregnant.

In an effort to cover up his adultery, David summoned her husband from the battlefield. David asked Urriah
about the war, then told him to go home to his wife.

He didn't go. Instead he remained at the palace with
the king's servants. When David asked Urriah why he had
not gone home, he replied that he could not do so while his
comrades in the army were sleeping in the open field.

David detained Urriah for another day, and then dis-
patched him with a letter for Joab, the commander of the
Israelite army—a letter which was in effect Urriah's death
warrant. In the letter, David instructed Joab to place Urriah
in the front lines of the fiercest battle and then retreat from
him so that he would be killed. Joab did so, and then sent a
messenger to report Urriah's death to David.

After Bathsheba had mourned for her husband, she
became David's wife and gave birth to a son.

At the Lord's direction, Nathan the prophet came to
David and told him a story about two men—one rich, with
many animals, and the other poor, who had only one small
lamb which he treated like a pet. When a guest came to the

---

528. 1 Chronicles 3:5

rich man's house, he refused to kill one of his own animals to feed the guest and instead killed the poor man's lamb.

King David was indignant at such villainy, and ordered that the rich man make restitution fourfold for what he had done.

Then Nathan declared: "You are the man!"[529]

Nathan went on to detail how David, whom the Lord had blessed abundantly, killed Urriah and took his wife. Nathan also pronounced the Lord's judgment: David would have war the rest of his days; evil would come against him from his own household; his wives would openly have sexual relations with another; and the child he and Bathsheba had conceived would die.

When Nathan finished, David confessed: "I have sinned against the LORD."[530]

Questions to ponder or discuss: How does David's response when confronted with his sin compare with the responses of Adam and Eve when God confronted them? Or with the responses of Saul when confronted by Samuel? Do you think Adam and Saul would have fared better with God if they had done what David did? What kind of repentance does God expect or desire from us?

---

529. 2 Samuel 12:7

530. 2 Samuel 12:13

Chapter 102
The Children of David and Bathsheba
(2 Samuel 12:15 – 12:25)

Not long after Nathan confronted David, the Lord made the child of David and Bathsheba very sick. David fasted and prayed, laid on the ground all night, and resisted all efforts to help him or raise his spirits.

After seven days, the baby boy died. The king's servants were afraid to break the news to him for fear that he might harm himself. But David perceived the truth from their behavior, and when they confirmed the child's death David washed, changed clothes, and requested something to eat.

His servants were astounded, for they had assumed that his despondency would only increase once he learned that the child had died. But David explained that he fasted and prayed while the child was still alive in the hope that the Lord might change his mind and let the child live. After the child died, all such hope vanished, as did the reason for the fasting and praying. David then added: "Can I bring him back again? I will go to him, but he will not return to me."[531]

David and Bathsheba would have more children, the first of whom was Solomon, which means "peace." This may signify that David had made peace with God, or it may refer to David's victory over Ammon,[532] which would have brought peace in a different sense. Nathan called the boy Je-

---

531. 2 Samuel 12:23

532. See 2 Samuel 12:26-31.

didiah, which means "beloved of the LORD."[533] Bathsheba
later gave birth to three more sons.[534]

Questions to ponder or discuss: David sought to change
God's intentions through devotion and penance, but it didn't
work. Why do you think it didn't work?

Have you ever tried to influence God through increased devotion, sincere penance, a special offering, a
promise, or something else? What happened when you did?

---

533. 2 Samuel 12:24-25

534. 1 Chronicles 3:5. Their names were: Shimea, Shobab, and Nathan.

Chapter 103
The Murder of Amnon
(2 Samuel chapter 13)

King David's oldest son, Amnon, was in love with Tamar, his half-sister, who was the full-blood sister of David's third oldest son, Absalom.[535] With the connivance of his cousin, Jonadab,[536] Amnon pretended to be sick and requested that David send Tamar to cook something for him to eat. When she came, Amnon raped her.

The Law required that a man be put to death for raping a girl who was engaged. (Deuteronomy 22:25-27) However, if the girl was not engaged, Deuteronomy 22:28-29 required that he marry her and never divorce her.[537] Tamar apparently was not engaged, for she unsuccessfully tried to talk Amnon into marrying her instead of raping her.

Amnon compounded his sin by refusing to marry the girl as the Law required. Indeed, he refused to have anything more to do with her.

---

535. See 2 Samuel 13:1. Absalom and Tamar were the children of King David and Maacah, the daughter of Talmai, king of Geshur. Amnon was David's son by Ahinoam of Jezreel, whom David married at about the same time he married Abigail. Absalom would later name his daughter after his sister, Tamar (see 2 Samuel 14:27), which is a good indication that he felt very close to his sister.

536. Jonadab was the son of Shimeah, David's brother.

537. Lest we judge this law too harshly, we must recognize that in that time and culture a girl who had lost her virginity would be much less desirable as a wife, and a woman with no husband would have difficulty supporting herself. Thus, the requirement that the man marry her and never divorce her ensured her survival.

Chapter 103 – The Murder of Amnon

When Absalom learned what had happened, he took care of his sister and contemplated how he could avenge her honor.[538]

Two years later Absalom saw his opportunity. He invited the king and all of the king's sons to a celebration of the shearing of Absalom's sheep. King David declined, but Absalom persuaded him to let Amnon come. During the festivities, Absalom's servants, at his direction, murdered Amnon when he was drunk.

Absalom fled to Talmai, the king of Geshur, his maternal grandfather,[539] where he probably believed he would be protected. He remained there for three years. During that time David mourned for Amnon, but longed to see Absalom again.

Questions to ponder or discuss: When King David learned what Amnon had done to Tamar, he was very angry, but he apparently did nothing about it. Similarly, David did not seek Absalom's return from Geshur so that he could be punished for Amnon's murder. As we will see in Part Two, David later urged leniency toward Absalom even when he was in open rebellion against the king.

When people obey the law (and I like to think most people do), do they primarily do so because it's the right thing to do or because they fear the consequences if they get caught? Would we learn from our mistakes if we did not suffer any consequences as a result? Why or why not?

---

538. 2 Samuel 13:20-22; 2 Samuel 13:22 merely says that Absalom "hated" Amnon, but 2 Samuel 13:32 indicates that his thoughts about vengeance probably began soon after learning of Amnon's mistreatment of Tamar.

539. See footnote 535.

Index of Biblical Books

(A page number in italics means the reference is only in a footnote.)

Index of Persons and Places

(A page number in italics means the reference is only in a footnote.)

Index of Persons and Places

Amalek/Amalekites	49, 50, 80, 101, 123, 127, 175-178, 197, 198, 201, 205-207, 209, 218
Ammon/Ammonites	8, 17, 86, 123, 137, 138, 162, 164, 168, 169, 172, 175, 203, 217, 218, 222, 224
Amnon	205, 226, 227
Amorites	*9*, 11, 86, 87, 95, 112, 114, 115, 119, 137
Angels	7, 16, 17, 25, 28, 29, *53*, 55, 88, 89, 127, 128, 139
Antioch, Pisidian	170
Aphek	197, *198*, 199
Aqaba/Gulf of Aqaba	84-86
Aram/Arameans	217, 218
Arnon River	86, 87
Asahel	206, 208
Ashdod	159, 160
Asher	26, *72*, 121, 132, *197, 203*
Ashkelon	140, *159*, 160
Baal-perazim	211
Baanah	*209*
Babylon (or Babylonia)	*12, 107*
Balaam	88, 89, *176*
Balak, King of Moab	88, 89
Barak	125, 126
Bathsheba (aka Bath-shua)	*196*, 222-225
Beeroth	109
Beersheba	164
Benjamin	26, 72, 115, 146-148, 165-167, 172, 197, 206
Besor, brook	201
Bethel	30, 164
Beth-horon	*172*
Bethlehem	144, 150, 152, 179, 181, 186, 187, *210*, 211
Beth-shan	203
Beth-shemesh	161

231

The Old Testament Made Simple (Part 1)

The Old Testament Made Simple (Part 1)

Index of Persons and Places

The Old Testament Made Simple (Part 1)

The Old Testament Made Simple (Part 1)

Index of Persons and Places

The Old Testament Made Simple (Part 1)

www.ingramcontent.com/pod-product-compliance
Lightning Source LLC
Chambersburg PA
CBHW051821040426
42447CB00006B/315